IN SEARCH OF THE BLUES

SOUTHWESTERN WRITERS COLLECTION SERIES

The Wittliff Collections at Texas State University–San Marcos

STEVEN L. DAVIS, EDITOR

IN SEARCH
OF THE
BLUES

A JOURNEY TO THE SOUL
OF BLACK TEXAS

Bill Minutaglio

FOREWORD BY
Linda Jones

University of Texas Press ᗡᗞ Austin

The Southwestern Writers Collection Series originates from the Wittliff
Collections, a repository of literature, film, music, and southwestern and
Mexican photography established at Texas State University–San Marcos.

Copyright © 2010 by the University of Texas Press
All rights reserved
Printed in the United States of America
Second paperback printing, 2010

Requests for permission to reproduce material from this work should be sent to:
    Permissions
    University of Texas Press
    P.O. Box 7819
    Austin, TX 78713-7819
    www.utexas.edu/utpress/about/bpermission.html

♾ The paper used in this book meets the minimum requirements of ANSI/NISO Z39.48-1992
(R1997) (Permanence of Paper).

LIBRARY OF CONGRESS CATALOGING-IN-PUBLICATION DATA

Minutaglio, Bill.
In search of the blues : a journey to the soul of Black Texas / Bill Minutaglio ; foreword by
Linda Jones.
    p.   cm. — (Southwestern writers collection series)
    ISBN 978-0-292-72247-7 (cloth : alk. paper)
    ISBN 978-0-292-72289-7 (pbk. : alk. paper)
    1. African Americans—Texas—Social life and customs.   2. African Americans—Texas—
Biography.   3. Texas—Social life and customs.   4. Texas—Biography.   I. Title.
    E185.93.T4M56   2010
    305.896'0730764—dc22

                                                                    2009044161

To Holly, Rose, and Nicholas

CONTENTS

FOREWORD by Linda Jones   ix

ACKNOWLEDGMENTS   xii

INTRODUCTION   I

PART ONE: THREE GENERATIONS

Hanging Tree Blues   17

Black Panther Blues   26

Texas Harlem Blues   38

PART TWO: COMMUNITY

Congo Street Blues   49

Free Man Blues   58

Sand Branch Blues   70

Fire in the Hole Blues   86

South Dallas Blues   97

PART THREE: THE MUSIC

Photochemical Blues   109

Searchin' Blues   115

Last Man Blues   129

Lightnin' Blues   141

Chicken Shack Blues   147

Fourth Ward Blues   153

Zydeco Blues   157

CREDITS   166

FOREWORD
MEDITATIONS ON MINUTAGLIO

I spent much of my career traveling the country and the world, writing stories about ordinary people whose culture and traditions did not fit the all-American mold. Many of my pieces were about the profound African American experience. And my best work came from the times I spent in inner-city neighborhoods where voiceless people and unsung heroes dwelled.

I sat with mahogany old men who held court under shade trees. I stood in traffic with bow-tied Muslims who hawked newspapers on streets named after Martin Luther King. I spent time with bona fide Rastafarians and with "dread heads" who were passing as the real thing. I lingered at church after church in search of compelling black preachers who had mastered the art of the "whoop." These stories were my preference and my passion—and, of course, being African American helped.

Many of the people whose lives I explored were so pleased to finally have their stories told by someone who looked like them that they were happy to provide access and information, to unfurl their sentiments, their hopes, and their fears. But that privilege, based on racial and cultural kinship, was nothing that I could automatically assume or take for granted: I was a black writer who worked for the white press, and many of the ordinary people whose lives I wanted to chronicle still questioned my motives. I had to work to earn their trust and gain their respect. In most cases, I managed to accomplish that.

So how did Bill Minutaglio, a writer who doesn't even "look like us," manage to travel into the African American community and accomplish the same thing? How did he manage to get people to talk to him at the depth and level they did? One answer might be that he is a masterful writer and storyteller, and someone who has a high degree of integrity that is not for sale. But Bill has another special quality as a writer that should not be overlooked. He is perceptive enough to know when and how to "stay in the cut."

Bill isn't the type of writer who strides into someone's life, or someone's community, with an aura of arrogance and media entitlement. Instead, he tends to keep his profile low and to humbly *insinuate* himself into a place.

We first met when we were reporting and writing colleagues, both of us trying to figure out the enormousness, the complexity of Texas. Bill has a penchant—one that, as he has acknowledged, sometimes borders on obsession—for writing about African American culture. When I first heard about the white writer who had this "thing" for writing about black folks, suspicions emerged. Because of unfortunate and frequent run-ins with racism throughout my life, I was constantly questioning the "ways of white folk," as Langston Hughes—the writer who lit the fire for Minutaglio's obsession—so aptly put it. I wondered whether Bill's real agenda smacked of opportunism and exploitation. I studied him, read him, talked with him—and my suspicions subsided. I found him to be a person who was sincere and whose writing was both honest and real.

I appreciated how he worked with people and how he respected their sensibilities. When he had to track down elusive and reluctant subjects for his stories, he was persistent but not pushy. He was patient and attentive, and his nonjudgmental attitude made people comfortable enough to speak freely. Even some who didn't particularly know him or hated what he might have represented opened up to him in spite of themselves. He didn't do drive-by visits to communities, to homes, to families in order to produce quick-and-dirty stories that were devoid of depth. The Bill that I knew went to places with plans to hang out for a while—often to the point of vagrancy—until he was "in the cut," until he found the truth, the stories that told what was really going on.

He reminds me of another good writer friend whom I met during my days as a reporter in Detroit. His name is John Sinclair, and he is internationally known for many things: during his legendary hippie-radical heyday of the late '60s and early '70s, John cofounded the leftist revolutionary White Panther Party, managed the MC5 rock band, became a celebrated political prisoner of the war on drugs, and wrote the incendiary book *Guitar Army*. John Lennon once wrote a song about him.

But the John whom I met and got to know during the late '80s and early '90s was a Beat-style poet and musician whose writings reflected his love of the blues and the culture of the people who gave it birth. I first heard John perform his work at a literary coffeehouse in Cass Corridor, on the seedier side of Detroit. In his poems about the Delta blues, which he laced with references to juke joints, fish sandwiches, and music icons of the Deep South,

John spoke in language that was so vivid, nuanced, and naturally delivered that I found myself squinting to be sure that the man I saw onstage was really white and not a black man with very light skin. John's writing was culturally on point, and, like Bill's, it was "in the cut." When I learned later that Bill had not met John, despite having been a distant fan for years, I introduced them, and they became long-distance correspondents. Knowing what I know about them both, I'm not surprised. What I appreciate most about my two special white writer friends is that as much as they apparently love my wonderful culture, neither has ever boasted of having best friends who are black. (Sparing me from hearing that useless claim makes them both keepers!)

In the end, Bill's sensitivities would serve him well during his time in Harlem, New Orleans's Ninth Ward, South Central Los Angeles, the south sides of Chicago and Dallas, and numerous other black enclaves. This collection, *In Search of the Blues*, is, in part, an acute meditation on the people who created the music he loves—but it is also a poignant narrative window into the soul of the African American community—a place so complex, so wonderful, and so real.

The work, like Bill, is in the cut.

LINDA JONES
April 10, 2009

ACKNOWLEDGMENTS

This book owes its existence to the brilliant writer, editor, and historian Steve Davis. He is a righteous soul who embodies the notion that creativity and selflessness are not mutually exclusive—in fact, I suspect he is so creative because he is so generous. I had stopped being a healthy skeptic a long time ago and had unfortunately trudged toward suspicious cynicism—and so I wondered, at first, why Steve would be interested in my old work. *What was his angle?*

Meeting Steve and collaborating with him (and getting to know his wonderful family) was like embarking on a process of remembering something important, of getting reacquainted with some forgotten ideals—like dusting off tools tucked up on a shelf and putting them back on the workbench. He had no agenda other than to help resurrect some stories he thought had merit. So, it's no surprise that Steve is also the best kind of writer—curious, thoughtful, adventurous. I believe he lives life that way: he cares for Mother Texas at a deep, elemental level, exploring its rivers and its bedrock—literally, Steve, like me, treasures the plume agate from West Texas and the rare llanite, studded with blue quartz, from an enchanted part of Central Texas, and he knows these aren't just rocks he is holding in his hands . . . they are so much more than that. I am lucky to have met Steve, worked with him, and benefited from his wisdom.

A special thank you to the many editors, over the years, who allowed me to pursue my work. Each of them is tied by the almost unlikely generosity they afforded me:

Ron White in San Antonio once told me that he liked me because the story we had agreed upon was never the one I eventually wrote for him. Being naïve, I thought he was being ironic, that he was mad at me. I finally got his drift—that stories are organic, they can't be predicted before they are written. The first time I wrote for him, he told me to ride the interstate in Texas and just look for things. No need to fixate on what was out there—until you went out there. What an extraordinary editor. The journalist Beth Nissen was an early role model and mentor. She encouraged me, and I doubt I would have written a printed word if not for her. She gave me direction, some sense of purpose, and confidence. Melissa Houtte was a wonderful editor who took many chances on me, who defended me, who indulged me, who created a supportive, humane environment. Other editors I have known were products of some management-training program, or some such thing, but Melissa instinctively knew how to connect with people.

I met the fine writer Mike Geffner through the mail and phone calls, and we became close friends without meeting each other for a very long time. There are those good, joyous moments when you bond with another writer—and that happened with Mike. He helped me, pushed me, gave me work—for no damned reason other than he is, again, a selfless angel. Where does that combination of literary eloquence and charity come from? He tells me that he just likes to help people, especially writers.

Tina Brown, who works harder than almost anyone, was also one of the most supportive editors I have ever known. Working with her, for her, was an extraordinary experience—she was the best, for so many reasons. Tom Watson, a dear friend, is the paradigm of calm, good cheer, and eloquence. He is editor as artist—seamless, seemingly effortless, and simply astounding at turning ordinary material into something you might want to read. From inception to final product, Tom seemed solely motivated by how to make the story better, how to protect you from yourself, how to make your work shine.

Mike Nahrstedt gave me direction, hope and a free rein. He challenged me and didn't blink when I went into full high-opera mode. He gave me a long leash and made my work so much better. I would like to thank Tracy Dahlby, the director of the School of Journalism at the University of Texas at Austin—he is a fellow traveler in journalism, someone I felt an instant kinship with, someone who possesses a great mind and wit. He is a journalist through and through—and the future of that craft is secure under his careful, thoughtful stewardship. Also at the University of Texas, Roderick Hart, dean of the College of Communication, and Lorraine Branham, former director of the School of Journalism, were beyond supportive—they had faith in me, and for that I am forever grateful.

Jon Karp is a genius, and I am not sure how the hell I ever entered his orbit—but I am glad he let me in. I am grateful to have had him as an editor.

The same extends to Rene Alegria—so humane, so kind, so supportive. There are many other journalists, friends: John Branch (one of the greatest editorial cartoonists in the history of that profession—and one of the most damned loyal friends anyone can ask for), Louie Canelakes, John Wilburn, Randy Eli Grothe, Bill Lodge, David Leeson, Christine Wicker, Anita Creamer, Mike Maza, Waltrina Stovall, Steve Ueckert, Bob Compton, Lorenzo Thomas, Earlie Hudnall, R. L. Griffin, David Maraniss, James Lee Burke, Buzz Bissinger, Mario Puzo, Scotty Ferris, Gail Sheehy, Sir Harold Evans, Dan Rather, Chuck Nevitt, Patrick Beach, Brad Buchholz, Peter Osnos, Steve Levin, Ellen Kampinsky, Jeff Franks, John Burnett, Rob Tomsho, Ross Ramsey, Dick Tarpley, Laura Jacobus, Buster Haas, Claudia Feldman, Harriet Blake, and many more.

Allison Faust and Theresa May at the University of Texas Press are offered my endless thanks for giving me the benefit of their extraordinary guidance and counsel. As with the other folks I have mentioned, they have the patience of saints and an innate humanity that tends to humble you. Many thanks to the brilliant copy editor Kip Keller; my respect and appreciation to the kind and masterful manuscript editor Lynne Chapman. All the staff members at the University of Texas Press must be thanked. They are treasures.

Rose and Nicholas are certitudes, among the only things in my life that have ever really been perfectly clear and holy. Holly Williams has watched over me (sometimes with alarm) and caught me over and over again.

She knows more about the way I turned, too often I suppose, onto the unlit road.

IN SEARCH OF THE BLUES

The author and blues musician Joe Cooper, 1985. Photo by Randy Eli Grothe.

INTRODUCTION

Bring me all of your dreams,
You dreamer,
Bring me all your
Heart melodies
That I may wrap them
In a blue cloud-cloth
Away from the too-rough fingers
Of the world.

—LANGSTON HUGHES, "THE DREAM KEEPER"

It was 1968 in my middle-class neighborhood in New York City, and a friend of mine was at the door. We were both thirteen years old. I stared at him through the screen as he stood on the steps and looked up at me.

"The niggers are rioting up on Linden Boulevard. You wanna go see?"

He was an Irish kid—everyone I knew was an Italian kid, an Irish kid, or a Polish kid. The family next door was Irish. Their old man was a New York City cop. Across the street was a family with thirteen children. They were Irish. Their father was a New York City garbage man. My third-grade teacher and her kids lived across the street from me. They were Italian. One of my best friends lived up the block. He was Polish. He and I used to ride our bikes in ever-widening circles outside our blocks. We would brush up against the St. Albans neighborhood—where Joe Louis, Jackie Robinson, W. E. B. Dubois, John Coltrane, Miles Davis, Count Basie, Floyd Patterson,

Fats Waller, and Ella Fitzgerald had lived. That place was where the "coloreds" lived—and most people I knew used the word "Jonesies" to describe black people. My aunt told us, one day, that James Brown lived in St. Albans. We would drive our 1960 Pontiac Ventura by his house on Linden Boulevard. His place looked like a castle with a turret, and we would wait to see whether it was true that he would come out front to hand out dollar bills to anyone who walked by. I also used to ride my bike to the nearby New York City Public Library branch, pedaling past the Mafia men in training who were hanging out in front of the basement pool hall and the pizza-by-the-slice places and the candy-cigarette-newspaper store run by a Jewish guy named Jack. The badass girl group called the Shangri-Las came from my neighborhood. One of my brothers, the story goes, dated one of them. They sang that anthem "Leader of the Pack." I used to watch the guys in front of the pool hall carefully as I made my way to the library.

One day, I spun a revolving rack of paperback books and came across a collection of poems by Ogden Nash. I liked it. They were fun, snappy, and they seemed to suggest something important, without really being all that . . . important. And I looked for other books that had short poems. I found a paperback by someone named Langston Hughes. How and why it was in this library had to be a testimony to a few things—the enlightened mind of the person running the place and, perhaps, a nod to the fact that things were changing damned fast. It was the sweeping era of white flight in New York. A twitchy something was out there—a mad distrust, and the thinnest veneer being put on impulsive evils and tendencies, as if people I knew had thrown a little jacket over their hatreds, barely concealing them, barely containing them. The middle-class, soigné assumptions were like old parchment on fire, pieces of some sort of bourgeois contentment, some sense of order and history and routine, just catching fire on the edges. Like paper slowly burning and the words, the certitudes becoming evanescent.

My father, I know, would have died if he had learned I had found some holy texts in the paperback rack at the goddamned library. He was raised in Italy, he used to talk about being hated by white people when he finally settled in the United States—and he and my mother still sometimes talked in Italian about "the American people." And they were consumed, eaten alive, by the idea that whatever it was they had settled into in this part of America was crumbling. The niggers were up on the boulevard. And as if I were doing something criminal, I kept coming back to read Hughes, and it was like hearing, feeling music: "I could take the Harlem night and wrap around you, / Take the neon lights and make a crown." Like hearing something that had been deliberately locked away, buried behind cement, steel, cold things. It was like some secret flavored syrup: "Take the Lenox Avenue busses / Taxis, subways / And for your love song tone their rumble down."

It was like summoning smoke, something over there that you had to at least pursue, even if you had no damned clue—and would never have a clear understanding. It called up so many nameless things, things outside my ken, my abilities: whispers, silk brushing against silk, the ominous clanking of chains, bittersweet dreams, aches, and stolen pleasures. I felt as if I shouldn't be reading it at all. As if I should look over my shoulder: "Take Harlem's heartbeat / Make a drumbeat / Put it on a record, let it whirl / And while we listen to it play, / Dance with you till day."

The kid on my front porch was impatient. I had been reading Langston Hughes. The kid was on the lower step, looking up at me. Through the screen on the door, his face looked like some perfectly ordered, mathematically constructed cobweb. I used to dream, looking out that door screen when it rained, and watch the way each little square filled with water, blurring the outside world.

"C'mon, do you want to go see the niggers?"

Martin Luther King Jr. had just been assassinated, and people had gone to Linden Boulevard in my changing, white-flight neighborhood, moving east from James Brown's house, from where W. E. B. Dubois had lived, from where the prophet John Coltrane had lived. No, I didn't want to go to the boulevard. What would I see, what would I ever know?

When I went to college, I lived in a part of New York some people called White Harlem. I walked north a few blocks to 125th Street and strolled around by the Apollo Theater. I went to the reopened Cotton Club. Langston Hughes had gone to my college for a while, until racism drove him away, until he began spending more time being interested in 125th Street, in all the streets of Harlem. I took a job monitoring free-food programs for the United States Department of Agriculture—and I would go to the World Trade Center offices of the USDA and get a list of churches, schools, and community centers in Harlem and the South Bronx and East New York. I would go to those places, day in and day out, to make sure that children—almost all of them black—were getting a "super doughnut" (one injected with vitamins), which the government was handing out. It was a more elemental education than the one I was getting at my Ivy League university in Manhattan. I took long subway rides, the only white face on the crappy, bleak trains, and exited at stops I didn't know existed. I slowly walked up flights of subway steps and headed to the street, holding my breath, steeling myself against some fear and an abject, dizzying sense of entering some place that I shouldn't be in—because I would die, because I would be chased, because I would have to admit, on my damned knees, that I had no clue and would have to explain the millstone from a lifetime of inherited things.

I walked for blocks and blocks through a 1970s New York City that had been reduced to postwar rubble. Buildings with wings, floors amputated. Dozens of them in a sort of bombed, Dresden slouch. Some were cracked open, with walls exposed, as if you were looking inside a scorched dollhouse left behind in the ruins of an inferno. And when I walked by, inside the falling buildings all over East New York or Brownsville, I would suddenly see a child standing up, dressing, and staring into a mirror. An adult would appear, look through the dangling wires of the apartment building, and guide the child outside. The free-lunch man was coming. And it was time to leave this abandoned place, this place that should have been torn down, this place desperate people had decided to pretend was really a functioning home. In some parts of New York, some bureaucrat ordered landlords to paint windows on some of these condemned buildings. Some trompe l'oeil, pretend reality. So if you were walking by or driving by, the building wouldn't look abandoned. Fake windows with fake potted plants sitting under fake window shades, all painted in Easter-egg blue and red. I went to East Harlem and tried to fathom where my family's immigrant roots fit in, where the old Italian neighborhood in Harlem had gone. Langston Hughes had helped define the Harlem Renaissance, he had been all over this place: "The night is beautiful, / So the faces of my people. / The stars are beautiful, / So the eyes of my people."

And I sat by myself when I went to see Big Joe Turner in a club one night, and he leaned against a stool and paused before he began to sing. He was still large, still a commanding presence, but he looked as if he were posing for his final studio portrait, the sepia-toned legacy photograph, and it happened to be in this room, one like a million rooms from Kansas City to New Orleans, and his head was crowned by yet another undulating halo of cigarette smoke. If he had slowly drifted right up through the smoke and disappeared that night, transported by both his immense dignity and his profound weariness, I would not have been surprised.

On a summer break, I took a Greyhound to New Orleans and lived for a few weeks in a motel near the highway. I walked some streets near Congo Square, walked down Canal, and got lost well beyond the geography, never feeling so alone. Back in New York, I wrote something about the Cotton Club. I wrote about a sad family in Harlem whose daughter had been killed in the apartment building they lived in—and I never understood why they let me into their living room, why they opened the door. At night, I sat on a rooftop on an old building on Morningside Drive and looked down the hill, down into Morningside Park, into Harlem. There were fires, sometimes, and there was action on East 116th Street. And I thought long and hard about the fact that on my first day in the Ivy League there was an announcement—that you better not miss your subway stop, that you better not get off the subway in Harlem. What I didn't know, until years later, was that I was living in the building Langston Hughes had once lived in.

In the late '70s, I moved to Texas to work at a newspaper in Abilene—the only paper in the world with a quotation adapted from Lord Byron's *Don Juan* as its slogan: "Without or with offense to friends or foes, we sketch your world exactly as it goes." I ate my first barbecue at the wonderful Turnerhill's—and the nice man who ran the place told me there was an interesting black history in the city. Walking around one day, I found a record store called Brother's in that small zone that was clearly the black neighborhood. Abilene wasn't really that different, it seemed, from where I grew up in New York City. There were boundaries, real and imagined. I really wouldn't understand until later (and this was addressed in a good book by the writer Lolis Eric Elie called *Smokestack Lightning*) that barbecue in Texas, in the South, could actually serve as the great equalizer, the palliative. The smoke was some sort of healing incense that drew people of different colors together.

A year later I moved to San Antonio and spent a growing amount of time visiting the East Side. Tucker's Kozy Korner, which identifies itself as the oldest African American bar in Texas. The Web Lounge, where jazz and blues guys in the air force would jam with Clifford Scott, Spot Barnett, Jitterbug Webb, Rocky Morales, and the local gods and goddesses. There were the Cameo Theater, where Louis Armstrong played, Johnnie Phillips's Eastwood Country Club, the San Antonio Black Sox baseball team, the Carver Center, Inman's barber shop, the influential Sutton family. I walked the cemeteries on the East Side, walked along East Houston and East Commerce, by the grand homes on Dignowity Hill. At night, with the sun finally setting in August, I played basketball for hours at a park on a near East Side hill that felt like a good place for a stranger to feel elevated. Walking downtown one day, I found a poster nailed to a wooden building—it was for a long-since-gone Bobby "Blue" Bland concert at the Eastwood Country Club. I took it down and kept it until the day I was able to have Bland sign it for me. I drove my motorcycle, more and more, all over the East Side. It felt like New Orleans to me—drooping wooden buildings, vine-covered alleys, churches that tilted toward the street but that seemed to vibrate when you went by them on Sunday morning. Time had stood still—in good and bad ways. It was whatever comes well beyond bittersweet. Slice off the rest of San Antonio, and the East Side would have been what it was, what it was forced to be, what it sometimes aspired to be—a world, a self-contained universe, unto itself. You knew you had entered it. You knew you had left it. One day I was walking on the East Side again, and there was a blues mural up on a crumbling wall—some holdover from a show, a nightclub, some folk-art-like painting that someone had done that showed a woman on a phone telling someone to come on over. I asked a friend to take my picture next to it.

At night, I parked my car downtown and walked by the mysteriously potent Aztec Theater, the place that had a replica of a sacrificial altar inside. I would hang out in the pinball parlor on the corner, drink at the Esquire, and walk east. If I were lucky, the legendary George "Bongo Joe" Coleman would be out on Commerce Street near the river, setting up his big oil drums and then playing, rapping before jumping on his moped, a fez on his head, and zooming somewhere. And the East Side was just a few more blocks away, cut off, like most black neighborhoods in Texas, by the railroad tracks, by the highways.

A few years later, I moved to Houston—one of Samuel Maverick's descendants in San Antonio told me I would like it because it was the closest thing to New York in Texas. The way he said it suggested that I would find something there. I moved into a falling-down house across from the Fourth Ward, a dense collection of narrow alleys, shotgun shacks, poverty, and neglect. And I knew, from the days I walked and drove through that sad, neglected city within a city, that there was no doubt nothing like the Fourth Ward in America. Sitting in the un-air-conditioned This Is It soul-food emporium one 100-plus-degree day, looking at a black-and-white TV with tinfoil for an antenna, my head matted with sweat, I felt—maybe—that I was going to die. Smothered by the humidity, by the things pressing down. The cultural claustrophobia. It reminded me of the souks I had visited in Morocco, where you went deeper until you had no sense of direction and everything linear was turned feverishly serpentine. It was like being buried alive. The entire zone, all of the Fourth Ward, was clearly a plaything for the city's rulers, and they were hovering, far away, looking down at it. Too many things, too many people, had conspired to create the Fourth Ward as it existed right then. One day I watched a parade moving from the

Fourth Ward and under the roaring highways that had dissected and exiled the area—the marchers, dressed in Sunday best, were headed to a church downtown, headed to the Antioch Baptist Church, which the powers that be had tried to cut off with their highway projects. Isolate the people from their church—if you can't burn the church down—and the community will shrivel and die. In the Fourth Ward, people walked to their church even if they had to march miles in the brutal heat.

A smiling woman named Gladys took me one day to see the Houston hanging tree outside the cemetery reserved for the city founders—and to see the nearby hidden cemetery, forgotten in the trashed-out lots, where the first black men in Houston were buried. I also met Earlie Hudnall, one of Texas's most important photographers, and we walked together down Lyons Avenue—once a vital artery for African Americans in the Fifth Ward. I went back and forth on Lyons for weeks on end. And it was like walking up the subway steps. Dread, anticipation, not knowing, and then seeing a pile of tombstone rubble alongside an old rotting building . . . pieces of pale gray tombstones piled up like Indian oyster middens on a barrier island in far south Louisiana. And that time, Juke Boy Bonner, the soulful poet and bluesman, was inside my head, talking about "staying off Lyons Avenue": "Cause if you go there green, / Somewhere down near Jensen'll be the last time you'll be seen."

And I read Lorenzo Thomas's poetry and heard him talk about black Houston, about how he tried to save Lyons Avenue, make it a place for arts and culture and a renaissance—but that things, well, got complicated. And we talked, late some nights, at that rickety apartment I lived in across from the Fourth Ward. He was hip, he was laughing, he was absorbed with the musicality of poetry, the raw blues and hard jazz of Houston, and I wondered what he thought about the fact that the brother of a famous Texas bluesman—a sweet-faced angel of the blues, an elegant purveyor of whiskey dreams—had slipped into my bathroom and was selling lines of coke. One time, some people I knew were looking for some drugs, and someone at a Houston blues club told them about another man to see. That man said he "had to go into The Alley" and he pulled out a gun, tucked into his waist, and came back a long hour later. In Houston, Thomas made me think hard about the maybe obvious crossroads between street-level blues and poetry— it was what Langston Hughes had rendered so eloquently. Both poets had their ear to the ground, so close to the bottom.

Allen Ginsberg came to spend some time in Houston, and I was his guide when he wanted to hear some Texas blues. He had just put out an album of spoken, improvised blues. I went to pick him up at the bungalow that he had been given to live in at Rice University. When I knocked on his door, there was this jumbled, scary grunting, huffing, panting, and then a "MOTH-ERFUCKING GODDAMN HOLY HELL MOTHERFUCKER" scream came from inside. I feared the worst. I knew a little about Ginsberg, and I had been obsessed by him for a while. In college, I had temporarily moved into the building he had lived in, in the building where he and Jack Kerouac had hung out. I went to the bars they had gone to. And when his bungalow door finally opened in Houston, he was in his underwear, sweat dripping into his beard, his eyes glazed over, and his glasses tilted on his face. I hoped to God there wasn't an undergrad in the room.

"I just passed a kidney stone," Ginsberg said.

He laughed, got dressed, and said he really did want to hear some Houston blues. We headed for a place called The Groovy Grill and listened to a trio play Jimmy Smith chicken-shack jazz-blues. Ginsberg was happy. He had a bag with him at all times, like an old-fashioned doctor's medical bag, and in it were books. He would listen to something someone played, something someone said, and he would reach into his bag and pull out a book and read out loud. He liked The Groovy Grill. He seemed to like Texas blues.

Another day when I was on Lyons Avenue, I was hoping to make it all the way to the tasty Lockwood Inn, where Joe Semien made his barbecue. Some people called the Fifth Ward by its nickname, the "Bloody Nickel." Juke Boy said: "It's a struggle here in Houston, man, just to stay alive." I stopped in the hoodoo-mojo store called Stanley's House of Power on Lyons to buy knobby brown John the Conqueror roots, "goofer" dust collected from cemeteries, nails yanked out of old coffins, and to watch people write down their wishes-to-be on scraps of paper and slide them under some burning black candles in a back room. The day I was there, the guy who owned the place had put a Frank Sinatra album on a turntable. That was unsettling, and it made me think of how many times we had listened to Sinatra in our home in New York, as if Sinatra could provide an aural firewall that would cloister us against the niggers, the Jonesies, the coloreds, even Langston Hughes. When everything else seemed closed, shut down, boarded-up on Lyons, Stanley's House of Power was bursting with people whose bad and good intentions were painted on their faces like hopeful rouge.

I went to Mary's Place on Lyons, where a tabletop fan blew stale air and a jukebox played blues. I went to The Branding Stable, where I watched Little Milton recline like a blues maharajah on a couch with a well-dressed woman on either side of him. At the Club LaVeek, on Blodgett Street, guitar player

Johnny "Clyde" Copeland would go from table to table. At a mysterious house down the block, men in suits were constantly walking in and out and arm in arm with laughing women in tight dresses. There was Garcia's, a humble little club where Albert Collins and the musicians from Ray Charles's band would gather when they were off the road. And I would walk down Elysian Fields, down the blocks where I had gone to talk to the ethereal saxophonist Pharoah Sanders (he had exiled himself to Houston for a while, trying to get his act together, he said), to talk to the dignified singer Peppermint Harris, to talk to the massively intellectual jazzman Arnett Cobb, to talk to the manic bluesman Big Walter Price, and to talk to an old man who still played the bones—ham bones. I went to look for the ghosts at the El Dorado Ballroom, at Elgin and Dowling, where Duke Ellington had played. And I looked for them on Erastus Street, where the hustling kingmaker, player, promoter, and producer Don Robey ran The Bronze Peacock club. I believed Juke Boy, more than ever before, when he said: "This city's full of slickers, boy, so you better know what you're doin'. / 'Cause you know Houston— that's the action town."

After two years in Houston, I felt something emerging: almost every rural and urban racial puzzle in Texas could be seen through the filter of Houston—not necessarily understood, but it was a place to start. It was where people fled to, where people made a stand, where people were exiled to, where people grappled for some small inch of the gilded tent. The musicians tried telling me, but I didn't hear them the way I should have. Cobb and bandleader Milt Larkin tried. So did musicians who weren't from there but were defined by Houston, who really knew Houston and what it meant to be African Americans—artists like Johnny Otis and Etta James. In the back lot of JB's Entertainment Center, I sat on Bobby Bland's tour bus, and I had the feeling he was wondering why I kept appearing at every club he played in the state. He talked about Houston, about Texas, about how, as T-Bone Walker said, "the hustle is always on." Houston was close to New York in that way. And in the end, I listened to that city's forgotten Hop Wilson, and I wanted to believe his hopeful prayer about getting to move to that metaphoric Sugar Hill, about moving across the river, about just staying alive. His words could have been written by Langston Hughes: "I done got over, well, I done got over, well I done got over . . . done got over at last."

One time in Houston I was talking with Jean-Baptiste "Illinois" Jacquet, who is credited with one of the greatest sax solos ever recorded (on "Flying Home"). We figured out he was now living very close to my old house in New York, and I was living very close to where he had grown up in Houston.

I didn't tell him that we had fled the niggers, that I had tried to compre-hend Langston Hughes, that I had driven by James Brown's house to see whether he was giving money away. For a while, Jacquet put me on his Christmas card list.

I began to "specialize" in stories about African American culture, people, history, politics. Not that I knew anything—but because, to me, there was no one else doing anything at my newspapers. In Abilene, there was one black journalist. When I worked in San Antonio, there was a black photographer and a black sportswriter. In Houston and Dallas, it was pretty much the same. There were precious few "minority" reporters. In Dallas, I remember being struck, right after I arrived in 1983, that there was something called a South Dallas Bureau—as if that part of town were a foreign country. The woman who ran the bureau was a legend in the black community—and rightly so.

I spent a dozen years in Dallas, and early on, I walked on old Forest Ave-nue—some people said it was named after the Confederate general, Nathan Bedford Forrest, who massacred 300 black prisoners after the surrender of Ft. Pillow in 1864 and later helped found the Ku Klux Klan. Dallas was once the national headquarters for the Klan. That much I knew. And Forest Avenue eventually became Martin Luther King, Jr. Boulevard.

I stopped in a dry-cleaning store that had an intriguing name—Baccus. The owner, Jasper Baccus, chased me down the street in the direction of the fine old home where Stanley Marcus—who ran Neiman Marcus—had grown up before all the white families moved out of South Dallas. Baccus chased me almost all the way to the Elks lodge, threw my business card in the gutter, and yelled that nobody from any newspaper ever came to South Dallas. When I got back to the paper, I was told that he had called and asked whether I was actually an employee. He thought, I assumed, that I was a cop.

I spent years working on stories that centered on African American com-munities in Texas. William Snyder, a Pulitzer Prize–winning photographer, and I traveled the country for a series of stories about streets that were named after Dr. King. I talked to James Farmer, Jesse Jackson, John Lewis, Count Basie, B. B. King, and Ray Charles. I retraced the route of the Freedom Rid-ers through the South. I went back to Harlem to write about its future and its past. I wrote several stories about the blues in Texas, and I traveled to the Mississippi Delta several times and wrote about blues there. I went to Tunica, Mississippi, and talked to elderly women who lived in tarpaper shacks in what Jesse Jackson had called America's Ethiopia. I spent every day for a solid month, from sunrise to late at night, in an alley in South Dallas, trying to stay warm around a fire that had been lit in a barrel—there were homeless people, out-of-work carpenters, roofers, children, crack addicts, and even a wandering city councilman. I took notes, pooled money for forty-ounce bottles of malt liquor, tried to interpret people's welfare forms for them.

In New Orleans, I took a cab to the Desire housing project and watched young men pass packs of crack into car windows. I went to South Central Los Angeles and hung out with a man named Earthquake and other members of the Rolling 30s Crips. I went to Des Moines, Denver, Washington, D.C., and Philadelphia and spent time in neighborhoods, asking people about Dr. King's legacy. I talked with the head of the Junior Black Academy of Arts and Letters and got to be good friends with a man in Dallas who called himself the Right Reverend of the Blues. Often, I stayed up until sunrise at a famous place called The Green Parrot, in South Dallas, and talked with a music promoter and club owner named Earnest Davis. He once owned a nightclub called The Classic Club, which had featured the best blues players in America, as well as odd acts like a hulking man in a nice dress known as Mister Aretha Franklin. While a fine Texas saxophonist, the late Marchel Ivery, played one night, the singsong-voiced Davis challenged me to identify what car he was driving just by looking at his car keys. I guessed a Mercedes, and he bought me a drink and asked why we couldn't be real friends, why it was that we would probably never be real friends, why we would really talk, black man to white man, only at four in the morning in the supreme late-night nexus, at an after-hours room in deep South Dallas. He always insisted on walking me to my car. One time I was outside a place called the Blues Palace with that same Pulitzer Prize–winning photographer. A man with what looked like a machine gun was guarding the door. It was two in the morning and the club was emptying. My photographer friend said that it looked like a nice night. I pointed behind him at a large woman wearing nothing but panties and standing in the dirt parking lot, calmly talking to two men. The jazzman Ivery used to talk to me about "the night people"—how they were a demanding and sometimes surreal audience. It seemed like something Langston Hughes would know.

At home, my wife began talking about my "African American complex." And one day at the newspaper, I walked in on two editors. They were sharing a laugh. One of them said to me: "You know what people say about you? 'Wherever there are two black people, you'll find Bill Minutaglio.'" The reporter at the desk next to mine turned to me one day: "I like to go to West Texas. You like to go slumming."

In front of the newspaper, a leading black activist regularly protested the newspaper's coverage of various issues. After that black activist became an elected official, a county commissioner, he was involved in a fracas at one of his protests. I was at home, and the editor of the paper called me, saying the man would talk only to me. But why? In many, many ways, I didn't really want to talk to him—what would I know, do, say? What did I really know about anything? *What could I understand?* He had to know I was pretending, assuming too many things.

I won awards from black journalist organizations—national ones, local ones. And for years, I blanketed myself in some righteous robes and presumed that I was serving some higher goal. That I was doing all this because it was important for everyone else to know these things, these stories.

I once spent a seemingly endless sequence of Sundays going to black churches, one after another: tiny wooden churches that had twenty elderly people inside, and bigger brick ones that had once housed all-white congregations and were now exclusively African American. Often, I would be escorted to the front pew. And when I stood to leave, people would let me go first. Very rarely was I ever asked why I was there. At a church in South Dallas one summer Sunday, I almost crawled to my car after hearing the entire congregation locked into a hammering, intense rhythm that was unlike anything I had ever heard. It was beyond gospel. Something as hard as metal would have broken under the rhythm I heard, and that was, perhaps, its intent. When I was in San Francisco during that city's last great earthquake, a nighttime aftershock reminded me of that church—like something that had stolen into my room, a shuddering presence, like frames in an old movie suddenly, loudly stuttering and stacking up on one another. Being in that church had scared me in a different way. Five hundred people spoke with one sound, one idea spun straight from the kinds of truths that can emerge only from having endured aching cruelties. And the people were unquestioning, even welcoming—and polite enough to not laugh as I walked, weak-kneed, down the aisle and out to my car.

I suppose I felt something sincere. I presumed that there were people in Houston and Dallas and Mexia, people I had written about, who had become my friends—and maybe hadn't been kind to me just because I was writing about them. It was all some kind of tangle, part obsession, part devotion, part guilt, and all that white-man's-burden business. I took my toddler daughter to a gospel music show in a tiny church. I took my best friend to hear the Five Blind Boys of Alabama at Lincoln High School, where the price of admission was one canned good. We were the only white people there, and when the lead singer decided to come directly to us, to walk directly down our aisle and stand right in front of us, we didn't know what to do. As he was thundering, enraptured, I could see a possessed woman jump out of her chair and begin to dance on one foot. All that I could think of doing was to touch the hem of the singer's white suit jacket as gently as if I were touching a rose petal.

And I went to more clubs by myself, and bouncers with rifles walked me to my car at four in the morning. I met a young black man who was a promising writer, and I decided to be his godfather, his patron, his adviser. He showed me his diary, and I convinced some people to publish it. He didn't, in the end, like me very much, although I helped him get a book published about his life inside the madness of the heroin-mean streets of Texas. I think he thought I was viewing him in the same way Katharine Hepburn talked about the little brown babies in *The African Queen*—in that condescending, paternal, and pious way that colonialists have always done it, the way the great white liberals practice their sanctimonious anthropology. The way beneficent white journalists parachute into someone's world and then radio home for an escort out.

Nothing was really clear except that, really, change was slow—and achieving something tantamount to comprehension and context was like trying to hold smoke in my hands. Jean Lafitte and Jim Bowie were still here in bedrock Texas, and maybe they were still marketing slaves. It is deep in the culture, it is always there in the tree rings. You can search for the blues and you will find them—or they will find you.

A man named Donald Payton took me around Dallas one day. As far as I knew, he wasn't the kind of historian who regularly published in *The Very Obscure Journal of Things That Happened in the Past*. Seemingly self-taught, he was fighting to find things, pieces of black history in Texas that no one wanted known. It was always an uphill climb, not that that was unexpected, considering the color of his skin and the things he wanted to resurrect. Payton made me slow down by an old building in Oak Cliff, just down the road from where T-Bone Walker, who changed the world by popularizing the electric guitar, had lived—and where Lee Harvey Oswald had lived—and where Jack Ruby had lived. There was a rectangular, waist-high shadow on a wall. It was where the old colored water fountain had been.

Payton said, of course, that you had to look for the shadows and then decide what they really meant.

My family, back when I was growing up in New York, twice joined the white flight. We finally sold our home in New York City to a black family for about the same price we had paid for it decades earlier. It was a crushing turn of events for my parents. It changed everything, and I believe it helped kill my father. We sold our home the same year "the niggers were rioting" up on the boulevard—the same year that I got robbed by some black kids outside a Catholic church. We were gone by the time the elm trees changed color in the fall.

We moved to a leafy, airy place in the suburbs. I made a friend named Jack. He was the only black person in school. I was new, getting into fights almost every day, and we seemed to get along. I invited him to come visit me. He lived in a small, isolated pocket that I would later realize was like other places around America that African Americans sometimes call The Bottom or The Bottoms. A hidden area, a forgotten area, close to the heavy traffic, close to where water can rise. Close to where people were in the shadows—good people, bad people.

When he came to my house, I heard my mother answer the door. She told him I wasn't at home. I stood at the staircase and saw him turn his back and go away. I don't know whether he saw me.

These stories were written over thirty years in Texas. Some appeared in newspapers, some in magazines, some in books I have written. They have been edited and updated. They take place in Mexia, San Antonio, Houston, New York, and Dallas. They are a form of odyssey—a white writer's chronicle of things he heard and experienced in Texas.

My friend Lorenzo Thomas published a collection of poems called *The Bathers*. The title was a play on words—a nod to something elegant and refined, and a nod to the water cannons that he had seen trained on black Americans during the civil rights movement. Thomas, for one, taught me that things are never, ever what they seem in Texas. You can try to script things in black-and-white—but getting to each side, getting to sureties, involves a long march through the gray zone. Through shifting tectonic plates of distrust, hope, and fear.

T-Bone Walker, from Linden, Texas, became my favorite blues musician—and it wasn't just because I had grown up on Linden Boulevard, where the niggers had rioted, where everything had changed, where someone had tucked a book by Langston Hughes in the paperback rack. I headed out to knock on doors all over the bottomlands of Dallas, where he had lived and played. I went house to house down by the old Elizabeth Chapel, one of the oldest African American churches in the state. I walked the curving streets and asked people whether they had once known Walker, whether they could tell me anything about him. A woman told me that she had known him and that she also knew a lot of other things that were long dormant: about the grandmother who could talk to the spirits, who could find the bodies of young black men who disappeared inside the muddy, demanding swirl of the Trinity River . . . and all that that fetid body of water implied.

Walker sang about the rivers in Texas rising, consuming you. And he sang about the confusion, about what happens when you don't know "which side of life to choose."

He said this: "Fate's an awful thing."

PART ONE
THREE
GENERATIONS

HANGING TREE BLUES

My editor at the Sporting News, *Mike Nahrstedt, knew that stories change. That legendary magazine, the oldest sports publication in America, founded in 1886, was usually the bible for statistics, hard facts, scores. Nahrstedt and some others wanted narratives, longer pieces that would rival the ones in "Sports Illustrated." And they hired me, put me on a contract, even though I was not technically a sports writer. It was, really, what they wanted. And they told me to write about Ray Rhodes, a football coach who was in the national news a lot then. The premise was that he was the ultimate hard-ass, that he was almost ferocious in his work ethic, his intensity. That it was Ray Rhodes against the world. I was going to see him in Pennsylvania. And I was going to go to where he grew up in Texas, in the small town of Mexia.*

In person, he was coiled, angry. And in his old hometown, I sat in the archives room at the small local library and read dusty articles, journals, and diaries. There were things there, including old photographs of General John Pershing passing through Mexia and listening to a "colored" parson preach. There were hints of something brooding at the edge of town, somewhere in the direction of the Navasota River. I tried to study the clues that suggested someone in Rhodes's family had been lynched. And I tried to figure out where it might have happened. Almost by dumb luck, I stopped at a roadside juke joint, and someone there told me that he thought some members of the Rhodes family lived around a certain bend in the road. I knocked on the door of a fading wooden shack, and that is when the story really began: when a black woman came to the door and studied me through the screen, almost as I had studied my friend when he came calling for me to see the niggers up on the boulevard . . . up on the street where I had found Langston Hughes's poems.

This, it seems, is a good place to start. This loamy realm where the night sky is the color of iodine and fractured with horizontal lightning.

A tall, bony old lady is staring hard at me through the battered screen door of her very hidden country shack—a falling-down house that is a lopsided grin in a tangle of trees. It has hardly rained all year, but tonight, close to the dank banks of the sluggish, snake-laden Navasota River, there is a deluge.

And a white stranger is outside her door. Someone who has been inquiring up and down rural Limestone County about a cross burning on a lawn—and about a hanging tree. A stranger asking if seventy-five-year-old Gutherine Newton might finally be the one who knows where the mobs used to go. Where they would go to slip a noose around a black man's neck and watch as panic washed over him.

In the nearest place that passes for a city—the weathered Central Texas town of Mexia, several miles to the north—there is a forgotten text in a dusty back room of the often-deserted municipal library. The small history tract says that well over a century ago, a man named Norville Rhodes was dragged to the hanging tree. A hanging tree close to Gutherine Newton's shack.

For a second, the suspicious woman, her face half hidden behind the screen, is quiet. Then she slowly reveals that she married into the Rhodes family. Yes, she knows about a tree. No, she doesn't remember someone named Norville Rhodes. But, yes, almost every Rhodes near here has been blood-related through the decades.

"I am Raymond Rhodes's aunt," she finally offers. "Raymond's daddy was born around here. You know Raymond Rhodes, don't you?"

She pushes the screen door open and steps into the downpour. She points me to a narrow country lane. She knows about a tree. People don't talk about it anymore; some people wonder why it was never taken down, chopped to the ground, with just aching moonlight guiding the work, with just some dairy cows standing perfectly still and thick and wide-eyed, staring through the rusted links of a barbed-wire fence. Why was that tree still there?

"Look beyond the bend. It's close to the road," the old lady tells me.

My windshield wipers struggle to shove sheets of rain. The road, choked by weeds, curves north past four trailer homes and a fire-gutted clapboard bungalow. Through the water-mottled windshield, a solitary presence takes shape. A thick-trunked tree. A tree, set off by itself, that looks like no other in the vanished community of Springfield. On the outskirts of Mexia—a place pockmarked with rusting oil-field equipment and empty lots—Springfield is missing from maps.

But the Texas hanging tree, outlined by weak headlights, is still here. This is the ancient place to start.

It is a moist, pregnant day, hundreds of miles away, and his feet are sinking into the lanky waves of Bermuda on the Philadelphia Eagles' practice facility at evergreen Lehigh University. We're standing inches apart. Ray Rhodes is staring—as hard and cautious as his Aunt Gutherine behind the screen door in Springfield, Texas. "You know, I'm not one of those guys who talks about 'payback this,' 'payback that,'" Rhodes says after dispensing with small talk. Already, he is remembering what he wants to remember.

Eight months earlier, after the Dallas Cowboys beat the Eagles, in the playoffs, Dallas coach Barry Switzer looked at the reporters and allowed his usual jack-o'-lantern slash of a smile to cross his face. "We kicked their ass," he gushed.

Rhodes studied the newspaper. He let the four words settle over him—over Raymond Rhodes, the not-quite-six-foot, forty-five-year-old overachieving man from Texas who somehow had become one of the only black coaches in the NFL, who had become the NFL's coach of the year at the end of his rookie season. Maybe he put the paper down. Maybe he picked it up again. He could almost hear the buzzing voice of Switzer, the bootlegger's son. That redneck yodel. He had grown up in Texas with people like Switzer. Rhodes neatly cut the article out of the paper and kept it in a safe place; maybe it would come in handy the next time.

Eleven days later, Rhodes spoke to Switzer through a Philadelphia reporter. "He will wish he never said that and soon. Paybacks are a bitch, man. It's something I will never forget . . . Switzer's gonna get his, man . . . You don't say [bleep] like that about Ray Rhodes and my football team. We're gonna settle this one. Real soon."

"You know, I grew up in a working-man's town. As a kid, my father instilled a lot of values in me. One of those things was respect . . . to treat people as you want to be treated," Rhodes says to me as he keeps one eye on his players slogging off the soggy practice field and trudging toward the locker room. He studies me, and I assume he knows I wasn't sent here to write about just football.

His hands on his hips, he stands with his right leg crossed over his left. He looks like a country kid in Mexia—"Ma-hey-yah," as the locals say—watching the curling Southern Pacific trains. Watching the dreams on steel wheels blowing by on a hot day in the boom-and-bust oil town, a place where the blacks still live on the west side of those tracks.

"Respect. This is something I've tried to live by. Do you know what I mean?" he demands. He waits for an affirmative reply from me while he rocks his body. As he is lecturing me, a light drizzle comes down. Rhodes ignores it. He likes to talk about Mexia. About how his best friend—his father, Thedford—grew up in the secluded Springfield neighborhood, out where the hanging tree still has some boards tucked up high among the limbs.

His body visibly softens as we steer toward the rural reference points. In the 1950s, there was dirt-yard football. The bittersweet cotton farms. The black preachers in starched shirts. The white oilmen slowly turning the street corners in long air-conditioned cars. It was like some endless Texas dream, a place he was assigned to be, a place where he would inherit his spot in line. He saw it all unfold for his parents, for everyone else. He wondered whether there was something else. "Everyone dreams. People dream about being successful. I was a dreamer myself. You know how it is when you're young? People tell you that you can't do this and you can't do that?" he asks me.

The rain comes down harder. The man from Mexia doesn't budge. It has to be deliberate defiance. He wants me to be drenched, to be off balance. It has to be that. He doesn't ever talk about the deep details of Mexia, Springfield, and the things that his Aunt Gutherine believes she sees around the twisting country roads that all seem to spill toward the river bottoms. "When they find a machine that can measure your heart, I'll be the first one to buy one. I'm never going to let people tell me what I can or can't do."

By now, the raindrops are popping and dancing off his windbreaker. "You know, I think this is still America. It's still a free country, and people are going to make the comments they are going to make. But the only thing I know is that those people, they are going to see me again," says the coach from Texas as he finally turns away.

"They are going to have to see me again."

Ray Rhodes told his family that he was putting his Coach of the Year Award in the basement. The son of a man who had spent years owing his soul to the J. C. Penney store, Ray Rhodes quietly told his friends that he still wanted to be more like his dignified father in Texas. His entire life, he said, had to be defined by a rigid demeanor—in the face of either easy triumphs or the yowling dogs of self-doubt and racism.

His father, the assistant manager at J. C. Penney, was one of only five blacks who worked in downtown Mexia. He and his wife raised three boys and one girl. There were hand-me-down books at the black schools. Long waits at a doctor's office while sick white children were treated first. And Thedford, Raymond's father, "urged" him to be the first to integrate the local white high school. When it came time for Raymond to transfer, he didn't know what to expect. His older brother Robert did. "It was back in the days of the cross burnings . . . Cross burnings were everywhere," remembers Robert.

A cross was ignited in front of the house where their mother still lives. Someone—they never knew who—put it there in 1967 after Raymond integrated the high school. And even if they suspected worse had happened in the past, even if they felt as though some other history coursed through the family, some things were kept hidden. His mother and father passed down many things, but they were reluctant to pass down everything: it wasn't until the brothers were adults that they finally heard the stories about Norville Rhodes, the man who was taken to the hanging tree at the side of that winding narrow lane in the soggy lands that spread out from the dark swirling waters of the Navasota.

Ray Rhodes, a star player for the Mexia High School Black Cats, was close to most of his black and white teammates. But his uncle Zeke, his father's brother, remembers taunts from the stands. "Sorry-ass nigger," somebody would yell when Rhodes slipped on a punt return. A booster club member deliberately tried to hurt Rhodes during an adults-and-kids scrimmage.

"Right will always win. Ignore it and go on," his uncle cautioned him one day.

In the fall of 1967, Hurricane Beulah spawned 115 tornadoes, and in a little Texas town, a boy who loved Gale Sayers and his mother's green peas was nicknamed "King of the Rhodes." Ray Rhodes "sloshed, skidded, slipped, slid, almost lost his balance on the wet field, darted, twisted away from tacklers, and finally almost everybody, including his interference," said the *Mexia Daily News*. In private, the old men on the black side of the Southern Pacific tracks said that the boy's abilities, his patience, helped steer the town clear of big racial eruptions. "The high school integration? That was a decision that my dad helped me make. I had to leave a lot behind," Rhodes tells me. "There are decisions when you have to do a lot of soul-searching, and you might shed some tears. When I was growing up, it was kind of tense. There were a lot of things going on in the country. But you had to tell yourself, 'I'm bigger than that. I'm just going to keep doing things I know are right.'"

Now, Rhodes is shaking his head at me.

"I'd like to try and not even put all that in this story. There are a lot of youngsters back there, and I want them to focus on the positive things about Mexia," he says in a grave voice. I knew that at some point in his life, he was told about the secrets in Springfield, the things that were deliberately not often named. He ran hard, he did his twisting and darting, and he went into adulthood with a reputation for having an unforgiving nature—for being someone who seemed to remember every perceived insult. He must have wondered how many hanging trees there really were in Texas.

He had left Mexia to play, unglamorously, for Texas Christian University, the New York Giants, and the San Francisco 49ers. At the end of Rhodes's playing career, in 1980, he was offered an assistant coaching position in San Francisco. There were no guarantees. It was, essentially, a part-time job. His bosses liked that Rhodes had come up the hard way from Texas. Rhodes was quickly made a full-time defensive-backs coach. Finally, he was approached by Philadelphia; they wanted to talk to him about being their head coach.

That first meeting between the man from Mexia and the owners from Philadelphia began in a hotel suite in Florida at seven one evening. Rhodes did most of the talking. He was intense, coiled, the words coming in bunches. He began by talking about obsession. Then about adversity. "My thing is about how to overcome," Rhodes said.

After midnight, Rhodes finally left.

The next day, over coffee and juice, Ray Rhodes from Mexia, Texas, was made head coach. Then, four games into Rhodes's tenure, the Eagles were 1–3. In a humiliating loss to Oakland, they had meekly surrendered after being physically overpowered. On the endless five-hour flight home, Rhodes called his players down the aisle. He wouldn't admit it to many people outside the team, but the loss had taken more out of him than any game in which he had ever been involved. And, one by one, he told the players how painful it had been. Then he summoned each of his coaches, most of whom were young, professional unknowns, to the seat next to him.

The Eagles finished the year 10–6. Rhodes was named the NFL's coach of the year. Some people said he would be satisfied, at peace. Surely, he would be at peace.

The third black head coach in modern NFL history was making more headlines. Rhodes liked to talk about guns, about weapons, about fights in the street—about fighting because people were trying to hold him down.

At a team meeting the night before a regular-season game with Dallas, he stood up and said:

"If the Super Bowl was going to be decided by a one-on-one fight between coaches, then the Eagles would be champions."

The players stared at him.

"He is why I'm here. I really want to go out and do my best for him, almost more than myself," star wide receiver Irving Fryar tells me as we walk off the practice field and beads of sweat flip off his eyelashes. "It's nice to see African Americans prosper the way he has. You don't have a lot of black coaches in the NFL. And him winning coach of the year? That makes him second to none. When you study the history of guys like him, you realize they have overcome a lot. I respect that."

Late one day, on the way to the parking lot and his car, Troy Vincent—who last played cornerback for the legendary Don Shula—is describing to me why he told his agent to get him away from the Miami palm trees and onto Ray Rhodes's team in icy Philadelphia. "Ray was the factor, Ray was the factor," he repeats. "Hey, I'm not going to shy away from this—I'm happy to see any African American as a head coach. For so many years, they have always been the assistant or coordinator. I know the history. I know what he and other guys have gone through. He has made history. To be honest, it makes you want to play harder for him."

One day, Rhodes tells me he is thinking about calling his mother, who still lives on Echols Street on the west side of Mexia, to check on the progress of the house he was building for her in a nice part of town. "I'm not a city boy," he tells me. "I'm a country boy and proud of where I'm from. I stay within my limits. When I played for New York City, I stayed as close as I could to Mexia—I got a home in New Jersey. I wasn't getting a penthouse in Manhattan."

When he is in Mexia, he walks the streets, where the West Side Crips have spray-painted their calling cards ("Crip'n ain't easy") on the abandoned buildings. An agency called Dads Against Drugs has moved into a cottage on his mother's block. Nearby, Burns' Diner, Uncle John's Swap Shop, and the Gemini Barbers are boarded up. Some older people walk by the shuttered businesses and linger for a second, as if hoping the places will magically open up again.

On the practice field, Rhodes insists to me, "I don't feel any different now than I did back then in Mexia. Sometimes, you feel like you're the underdog in every situation. I've always felt that I've had to fight an uphill battle. I'm not a hard-ass. I just don't want to hear how tough you have it. I want to hear how you're going to get out of that problem. If that's being an ass, then I'm going to be a good ass."

He stops abruptly.

"You know that story about the young kid who gave the elephant tobacco?" he asks quickly.

"That elephant got all drunk and stirred up. And then, twenty years later, the boy comes back to see the elephant. You know what happens, don't you?"

I shake my head weakly, not sure whether this is going to be funny. As he tells the story, he is crackling with enthusiasm. Most of the players, coaches, trainers, and hangers-on have abandoned the field. But Rhodes is still in the middle of all the dampness. All the somber, leaden humidity and heat. Maybe it feels like a hot day thirty years ago in Mexia. Maybe he is remembering the tender mercy of a cool breeze, waiting for it the way people from both sides of the tracks did. And maybe he is remembering the legend of the doomed Norville Rhodes, or a lifetime defined by all the things and people that pursue him.

"OK, let me tell you what happens to the kid," Rhodes finally tells me. The outline of a smile begins to form on his face. "The elephant kills him. Dead."

And now, Ray Rhodes is close to grinning. He is gnawing on my discomfort. He is enjoying the fact that his story has pulled into the station with an off-center, bloody ending.

"So, you know what I mean?" asks Rhodes, almost laughing. "That's me. I'm the elephant. I don't ever forget."

This, it seems, is both a good place to start and to end. The big Texas lightning is still whipsawing through the warm night air outside Mexia. Gullies of brown water are sliding into the Navasota River. It is scary out here, perhaps because of the things unseen. Rivers rise unexpectedly in Texas. Rain-pummeled weeds are bowed down. In her lopsided home, Gutherine Newton looks tired.

"Raymond made us proud," she says. Her house looks tired, too, as if the beams, the shoulders, are sagging, as if the house is receding into the earth, rusty and eroding, like old farm equipment sinking into the soil, to be consumed by Johnson grass and vines and weeds and hovering trees. She doesn't want to talk about cross burnings or ancient lynchings at the brooding oak tree that is just out of sight but probably never out of mind. She says she doesn't know why that tree was never chopped down. Maybe, she says, people left it there to remind themselves.

"People remember what they want to remember," she tells me as her beat-up screen door slams shut and she disappears back into her home buried in the Texas woods.

Ray Rhodes went on to coach with the Green Bay Packers, Washington Redskins, Denver Broncos, and Seattle Seahawks. He is still considered, among football people, one of the most intense, uncompromising figures in the game. In 2008 he was hired by the Houston Texans as an assistant coach. In a way, he had come full circle, back to Texas, back to the things that defined his family. The hanging tree is still on the outskirts of Mexia.

BLACK PANTHER BLUES

By the early '80s, crack had officially taken hold in Dallas. I lived in South Oak Cliff, and when I went for a walk with my dog at night, there was repetitive gunfire—from automatic weapons—coming from an apartment complex just a bit farther south. The abandoned house across the street from me was being used to store stolen cars. Another house down the block was peppered with bullets one night, leaving the front of the place pockmarked. Someone threw a bottle of lemon-flavored wine through the window of my car when it was parked in my driveway; a neighbor rang my bell in the morning, thinking that I had been shot.

Once, I was in Americus, Georgia, working on a story about Dr. King and talking to a man who told me that he had jumped into the Mississippi River to rescue a young white girl, and that when he brought her to the riverbank—the fear still in her eyes, her breath still edgy, her mouth still spitting water—her kinfolks, her father and mother, took her from the black man's hands and walked away without saying a word to him. My phone rang, and it was my pregnant wife in Dallas. Someone had tried to break in the house, she had called my best friend, and he had raced over with a baseball bat—at the same time the cops arrived.

Not far from where I lived, Fred Bell had changed his name to Fahim Minkah and was trying to chase the crack dealers out of the neighborhood. Writers often called him when they needed a quote from someone who was pissed off at white Dallas. He knew the game and how it worked. I wanted to walk with him, go out with him as he tried to chase the crack dealers away. He told me to come to his house. He was working on a car in the driveway. I assume he thought I was another fake from the FBI. Or at least some kind of fake. We talked and agreed to meet at his next march. I went, walked, and interviewed several other people who were with him, including, surprisingly, one lone teenager. Minkah and I met several more times, and again I assume he knew exactly whom I had been talking to, exactly where I had been going. The sense I got was that he had spent years being more than careful, more than wary. And that he had deep roots all over the city, he knew who ran things, he knew about the alleged gangster Chicago Red, he knew about murderous cops. And I also felt that he knew he was getting older, and that he seemed inured to blowback. He had the air of a man who was no longer worried about rolling the dice with another white guy asking too many questions. He put up with me and, as he had done so many times before, hoped for the best.

Fahim Minkah lives his life minus one eyebrow, though most people don't notice unless he points it out. What was really obvious to me—what the self-satisfied, crack-dealing "rock boys" stare at—is the jagged scar across the meaty portion of his face.

Tribal looking, it stutter-steps its way from under one eye, slices across his nose, and ends in a cushiony spot on his cheek. Late on a hot Saturday afternoon, a couple of well-fed dealers are getting a chance for a nice look at it. They are getting a good look at Minkah as he stands before them at one of those do-it-yourself car-washing emporiums. His red shirt is matted to his chest. There is a thin layer of sweat on his forehead. Over by the mangled vacuum machines, Bennie and a favorite crack ally, a reed-thin teenager, are smirking at Minkah.

They are leaning against the open doors of their new candy-apple red Mustang. They have left the motor and the air conditioning humming. Ten feet away is the path leading to the omnipresent vacant field. It is the crack field—a forest really. Ringing it and deep inside it, the caked earth is littered with white plastic packets still coated with thin smudges of crack. All day, all night, people disappear in and out of that forest. People who know it, who know it really well, can step up to the edge of the inner-city forest, stick two hands into the mess of bushes, and then fan their hands apart, as if they are swimming, and find a hidden path through the thick, choking weeds and rotting trees.

It is humid and it feels dizzy hot, the kind of heat that makes no sense, that hangs on you like some stranger's insistent hand, that has an acrid taste like a copper penny.

"I am here," booms Minkah. "If you push drugs, you are my enemy."

Bennie laughs and plays with the chunky chains of shiny gold around his neck. Like Winston and the other big dealers who work the Oak Cliff neighborhood, he must have heard from the kids who run the streets for him: there is a loud, tall, sturdy brother making noise about chasing them away from Sunnyvale Street. They are making a rare appearance to see for themselves.

"If you can't make it rain," shouts Minkah, "I do not fear you."

Still chuckling, Bennie steps into his car, and his boy slips it into first gear. Kids love his car. And when kids like something, it instantly gets labeled "dope." An Armani suit is a dope suit. There are dope clothes. Dope shoes. Dope sunglasses. Bennie has a dope car.

Sitting with me in the front seat of his own car, Minkah notices, in a corner of the rearview mirror, that he is being watched. For the last minute, he has been staring at the mirror and rubbing a makeup pencil above his right eye.

"I lost my eyebrow in a car wreck," he says without turning. He continues to pencil in his fake eyebrow.

The scar?

"Somebody came at me with a knife," he says.

Minkah is about to make his rounds, snapping pictures and making notes on the crack-selling "flyers" who are swarming Dallas's neighborhoods. It is something he has been doing, by himself and with friends, for the last two years. And he is also about to encounter the one thing—he fears no human—that just might scare the hell out of him: the possibility that an original street-fighting man like Fahim Minkah can't get people to march along with him. Back in the late 1960s and early 1970s, he was a young black Orpheus. A political poet and urban magician. Head of the Black Panther Party in Texas, he was muscular in body and spirit. He had hundreds of young people in tow. The pews were jammed in handsome Fahim Minkah's cathedral of revolution. But now, in 1989, he has assigned himself a narrower, ultimately uneasier mission.

He is not, as he once was, directly confronting the mostly white plutocrats. Instead, he is plotting attacks against the black crack dealers who live and work in black neighborhoods. And without ever admitting it, he has also inadvertently presented himself with another set of orphic tasks: To determine whether people will still follow Fahim Minkah or whether he will have to walk alone. To determine whether young people will respond to a fifty-year-old black man's message. To see firsthand whether the righteous zeal of social consciousness, the pure 1960s zeal, means a damn to the kids whose lustful stares are reflected in the conspicuously consumptive shine of Bennie's dope ride.

When he was doing time in Leavenworth on a bank robbery charge, there were heavy cellmates, inner-city warlords who had kidnapped and tortured cops who got too close to the heroin traffic. "Those were some serious brothers," says Minkah as he backs his car away from the parking space in the Prince Hall Village apartment complex. By implication, he doesn't have much respect—or fear—when it comes to today's breed. Nobody pays Minkah to track Bennie, Winston, and the crew that has taken over the large abandoned field off Sunnyvale. He does it, in part, because he has always been outdoors, always driving, looking, striding. Before he changed his name, he was Fred Bell, Dallas's "most dangerous militant," according to one of the hundreds of internal memorandums written about him by the police and the FBI.

In the 1970s, when he helped head the Black Panthers in Texas, he decided to remain in the public eye even though he was never much for leading marches and chants. What he has always believed is that you must protect and police yourself and your own people. It was a lesson hammered home by the national wing of the Panthers. They took the law into their own hands after they became convinced the law wasn't helping and was, in fact, destroying their communities. Across Texas, Fred Bell helped lead boycotts and establish schools, dental offices, pest-control plans, food programs, health clinics, and community patrols. And a full decade before it became a burning issue at the end of the twentieth century, Bell was calling for deep changes in the handling of alleged cases of police misconduct in Dallas. He pored over the Dallas City Charter and found an obscure section that would push the Dallas Civil Service Board to examine charges against a city employee if four citizens filed a complaint. That discovery forced the board to schedule hearings on police misconduct—until an amendment was added to the city charter in the next election to eliminate the exact section the Black Panthers had exploited.

By the late 1970s, the national Black Panther party, with dozens of members dead or imprisoned, had begun to fade. Party leaders elected to retrench, and they summoned Fred Bell to the national headquarters in Oakland, California. He wanted, instead, to stay in Texas. And Bell, a rare black militant in one of the most racially tense American cities, resigned from the Panthers and became a Muslim car mechanic named Fahim Minkah. He had children and moved to the peaceful, airy southern edges of the city.

During his "rest period," as he calls it, he waited: "I'll come back when there are some other younger brothers and sisters with that gleam in their eye. I'll be their mentor." He waited but never saw enough of the gleam. And when the new breed of drug warlords got close to his home, he made a deliberate move back to the streets. Back to areas he knows better than most police officers, politicians, and journalists. He has lived in the infamous West Dallas housing projects. He has owned a car repair shop hard in the troubled heart of South Dallas. He was one of the first black men to walk the downtown streets of a Texas city with his angrily clenched fist raised high, leading hundreds of grassroots supporters who were demanding changes.

So, Minkah began trailing the crack prescribers, including the ones who lord over the litter-strewn acreage east of the carwash on Sunnyvale. The battlegrounds are, like many urban war zones, found on a block, on a patch of land, in a building. They are well defined, but only by people who live nearby. For anyone else, it is just a block, a patch of land, a building. Minkah knows what he is looking for. He jots down license-plate numbers and names. He patiently waits for his snapshots to come back from the Eckerd drugstore up on the corner, and he takes the pictures and he commits the faces to memory.

In 1987, he found some office space and sat before people in the neighborhood and asked them to join his new group—the African American Men Against Narcotics, a group desperately trying to reclaim South Dallas. He liked the way it sounded: AAMAN. It sounded like "a man" or even "amen."

One day, he walked out of the community center in the Prince Hall complex and found eight dealers fanned out before him.

"Well," Minkah said to himself, "I'm fixin' to have a confrontation on my birthday."

He had just turned fifty. There were sullen stares, long minutes, and unspoken threats. Minkah looked hard at each of the dealers. They left.

"The old dope dealers never wanted anybody to know what they were doing. Now, these dealers are so proud. So out front," Minkah tells me as he guides his car through the potholes at the Prince Hall complex. "They are being bold about killing our people." Outside the car windows, people stare back at us, their gazes lingering. He drives, patrols, stares back. Sometimes there is a connection, something as subtle as a nod. When he rides, he is hardly paying attention to the driving. The people who drive with him, the people who watch him, wonder just what the hell Minkah is really doing.

Toward the front of the faded apartments is a young, slim smiler leaning against a stone wall and wearing a blue Adidas jogging suit. As Minkah drives up, the man fans out four fingers at us like a third base coach sending in a signal.

"You got something for me?" yells Minkah as he sticks his head out the car window. His voice is full of genuine curiosity.

"Check it out," says the rock boy with an engaging smile.

"It's fixin' to get hot, brother," Minkah hisses.

The rock boy, still grinning, doesn't budge. Minkah opens his door, and the crack dealer glides backward around a corner.

Minkah drives on.

When the rock boys first settled on the corners near Prince Hall and began pumping crack to their chemical slaves—including the occasional white customers who drove up from Duncanville, Midlothian, and DeSoto—some liked to be rock ready. No vials, packets, glassine envelopes. Just a handful of rocks. Rock ready. If the headaches—the cops—arrive, you simply drop the crack and smash the rocks under your Nikes. But the cops hardly ever arrive here. So the little see-through envelopes with a thin red seal are the standard package. And today the customers, the smokers who are "on the pipe," have set up old chairs in the comfortable, shaded killing field off Sunnyvale.

Sometimes they bring portable radios, bags of food, and something to drink. They light up, and the curls of smoke ring the bushes and beaten-down trees. When strangers approach down the long main alley, they have more than enough time to disappear down secret paths through the hackberries and oaks. It is a Gordian knot, and it feels and sounds as though it is humming when you try to walk through the crack field. The cops don't run their big sweeps through here. This is not the immediate, stinging squalor of some parts of East San Antonio or the Fifth Ward in Houston. And that is ultimately why Winston and Bennie are here. That is why Minkah, who gets flagged down by rock boys twice every day, is here.

They know a simple something that the police and the occasional visitors can't seem to grasp. Selling crack is all about profit, and there is plenty of profit and not much hassle to be found in the well-populated, larger, seemingly quieter parts of a leafy zone like Oak Cliff.

It's three on a bright Saturday, and a steady, pleasant breeze is making the tree leaves chatter. When this part of Texas was settled, people came because there was cool, clear water in the little creeks and tributaries that curled toward the Trinity River. There were a few spots where the flat earth was interrupted by a bump and a shoulder, the land loped a little, and that made for some shade and for some breeze coming through the tall stands of oaks. It was good farmland, away from the river bottoms, away from the unrelenting flatness. The Tennessee settlers and the former Confederate soldiers picked their plots, started farms and dairies, and when their slaves died, they sometimes allowed them to be buried at the hem of the family plots. For decades—really, well into the early part of the twentieth century—this part of Texas, so close to a massive urban environment, was like some city on a hill that you passed from a distant road, some place with wooden church spires and white-columned homes set against the horizon. Oak Cliff was always the "Hidden City" in Texas—a place that almost became the most important city in North Texas, but that slipped into a jumbled state rooted in isolation, trickery, and fear. Oak Cliff became the least understood and arguably most complex part of Dallas, and everything about it flows from its early years, its history as a place where outsiders sought refuge and where ancient customs were held longer than they should have been. And today, this day, this moment, Fahim Minkah has inherited all of that hidden history. The airy, leafy attributes have been corrupted, consumed, and converted to something unyielding. The crack field was once a farm.

"Believe me when I say the danger is in Oak Cliff," Minkah lectures me. "It's more dangerous because the dealers are working near plenty more families, schools, and businesses." And so the rock vampires that haunt him are easy to find. They rise at seven to catch customers waiting at bus stops or traffic lights on their way downtown. They linger until well after the private nightclubs close down. Look near Prince Hall, at the Calvary Arms Apartments, at Highway 67 and Polk. Advertising, promotion, bargaining, and hustling are all in motion. Other things, too. Near Ledbetter Drive, some guys step out of a car. They calmly take aim at a new Cadillac, riddle it with bullets, and leave.

The cluster of pawnshops is always crowded. And late one Friday afternoon, two chuckling kids are leading a horse past some of the boarded-up windows in the East Ledbetter Apartments. It is like seeing a polar bear in downtown Houston. It makes no sense. It is a large horse, tethered with clothesline or the kind of rope used to tie a Christmas tree to the roof of a car. The two boys look like they are twelve years old. They run up to me at the stoplight and ask: "You wanna buy a horse? Fifty dollars." I go with them, and they walk the horse for me, as if they have done this a lot in the past. They sneak looks over their shoulders. They won't say where the horse comes from or why there is a horse in the jammed parking lot of an inner-city apartment complex.

And as Minkah swings his vehicle out of the Prince Hall complex, the Adidas rock boy reappears against the wall. Minkah waits for a gaggle of children passing in front of him. They are headed in the direction of the Elisha Pease Elementary playgrounds. We blend into traffic on Sunnyvale. As he steers, he passes the other rock boys the little children just walked by: the two walking into the big crack field, the one in the strip-shopping-center parking lot, and the three carefully cleaning their silver BMW in the carwash. Before people are swallowed up by the crack field, they sometimes linger for a second and look over their shoulders like people about to para-chute out of an airplane. If I blink, I will miss them; blink, and it is as if they were never there.

The only evidence of their passing is the embracing way the hackberries and the spindly bushes seem to fold back in on themselves, the leaves trem-bling a bit as if they are excited about something.

This is how one memorandum on Fahim Minkah reads: "[He] is a per-son around which a series of social controversies exist. He is a mature man . . . his experiential field points toward potential greatness or tragedy as he is the personification of a human paradox . . . the 'most' dangerous mili-tant in the Dallas area."

The memo was written years ago by officials at North Texas State Univer-sity (now the University of North Texas), people who were studying whether to admit Minkah—then known as Fred Bell. He wasn't let in. Fred Bell was a black radical with a criminal record. "Trying to assess what happened back in those days is incredible," Minkah tells me. He has a look on his face that says unless you lived it, you will never be able to even remotely understand or appreciate what it meant to be black and radical in Dallas in the late 1960s and early 1970s. He shows visitors the old newspaper clips. The one that lingers—beyond the clips about what might have been the first successful supermarket boycott in America and even the ones about a standoff with the police assault teams—is actually rather simple: the Black Panthers had set up headquarters in the West Dallas projects. Under Minkah, the party's strategy was rooted in a basic premise. Live and work where there are the most imme-diate problems. Several Panthers moved into the projects, organizing tenants and confronting apartment managers with rent strikes.

In the summer of 1974, the Dallas police, armed with a search warrant, staged a raid on the headquarters. They had been "tipped" that there were overdue library books in the headquarters. They turned the place upside down and found four library books. They weren't overdue. They became over-due, says Minkah, after the police confiscated them. There were other, more dramatic episodes. With members of the Student Nonviolent Coordinating

Committee, he organized a boycott against the OK Supermarket chain; the owners eventually sold the local stores to black businesspeople. He formed the Angela Davis Liberation Party and held "weapons and survival" training on land near Interstate 20. And there was the occupation of a Presbyterian community center in South Dallas, something people still talk about.

"The Dallas police had their tactical squad surrounding the center," Peter Johnson of the Southern Christian Leadership Conference tells me. "It was clear that Fahim was one of those people who will lay their life down at the drop of a hat." A negotiation to move the center into different hands was finally reached, and Johnson learned something about Minkah, something he believes to this day: "He is a hard-line brother, a real, real, hard-line brother. There aren't fifty brothers like him left in the United States. People who have gone—and will go—to jail for what they believe in."

It would be an unforgivable mistake, Johnson also tells me, not to appreciate the fitful length and breadth of Texas's bumpy road toward social equality. Without knowing that history, one might easily lump Fahim Minkah in the general pool of "Dallas activists." "Fahim is never going to get the kind of respect he's deserved from our people or from the majority. He was there from the beginning, before anybody else, and nobody knows what he went through. Here I was, an SCLC person, and they thought I was a house radical. Can you imagine what they must have done to him?"

The big thing "they" did was frame him, says Minkah. Convicted in 1969 of driving a getaway car in a bank robbery, he was given six years. He spent good chunks of the 1970s in and out of prison and in court contesting the charge. He insists to this day that he was set up and put away as a political prisoner, that his case was part of the extended, documented COINTEL-PRO (Counterintelligence Program), which was run by the FBI against radical and dissident groups. The program was designed to crush dissent in the United States and, by extension, to crush his version of dissent as head of the Black Panther Party in Texas.

When he tells me about having served twenty-six months of his life on the robbery charge, the drumbeats of 1960s rhetoric echo in the conversation. But two decades later, sitting in a folding chair in the garage of his pleasant home in the Singing Hills neighborhood, the terms he uses have a brittle texture to them. They are words as ancient talismans, vaguely ominous but ultimately impotent: agents provocateurs, freedom fighters, the exploited masses, concentration camps for political prisoners, guerrilla warfare, resistance movements.

"You know why Dallas never blew up?" Minkah suddenly asks me. "The preachers say they stopped it. Well, they lie. Some of the crowds that we faced down back then, if the preachers had gotten up there, they would have mobbed them. The people respected us. We told them we needed to train, practice, get the proper weapons and ammunition."

While their daddy speaks, his young children—he has four, ranging in age from five to fifteen—scamper in the front yard, singing nonsense songs and making sculptures in the mud. Things changed. Young radicals had children. They moved to suburban homes. Fred Bell became Fahim Jabari Minkah— the name means "intelligent, brave, just." The heat was turned down under the sizzling menace, though he continued to speak out at housing rallies, city council meetings, police review hearings, and even during a failed school-board bid. Today he remains convinced that the problems of twenty years ago—police corruption and brutality, political and economic racism—still abound for black Texans. Minkah may not exactly be living in the past, but he constantly, resolutely defines himself by it. He seems to need people to understand his present motivations by filtering them through his past inclinations. That wish is as plain as the scar on his face.

Saturday afternoon I watch as he sets up two big black loudspeakers at a corner of the parking lot of the Prince Hall apartments, opposite the giant crack field. The field, just a few feet away, is like the edge of some crackling fire in a landscape run riot, like something out of a J. M. W. Turner painting. Orange light is coming through the trees; there is a glimmer of metal as the sun bounces off the crack smokers' chairs. There is a rustle in the trees as the wind picks up the plastic bags, the crap, the refuse, and rattles it all around. The ground is strewn with condoms, rags, and those little glassine envelopes. The field, today, almost feels as if it is throbbing.

Minkah has just led a march of a dozen antidrug protesters down Sunny-vale and into the alleys that wind around the nearby apartment complexes. Those people—and twenty others attracted by something that promises a break from the aching monotony of the heat—are waiting for Minkah to speak. He has done this hundreds of times before, faced the bored, the hot, the barely curious, and their blank looks. Minkah is almost on his toes, leaning toward the crowd. He starts by saying he is setting up an office of the National Black United Front, a community-based activist group, in the Prince Hall complex. Then, of course, he mentions that he once commanded the Black Panthers in Texas.

"The only thing I have ever tried to do is save black people," shouts Minkah, his voice bouncing off the warm stones of the building and getting swallowed up by the crack field. "The government has compiled 2,165 pages on me. Why? Because I did the same thing then that I'm doing now. I'm trying to save people.

"We demand that the police department cooperate with us to get rid of drugs—or give us our tax dollars back. We are here to let you know that together we are strong. How much courage does it take for dope dealers to shoot kids?

"It takes courage to do what the Black Panther Party did in the 1970s. We told the CIA, 'Send an army against us, we'll just organize the people against you.'"

A few people in the crowd clap. Some nod their heads. Some walk away and disappear into the crack field. Minkah raises his fist in the air. When he does, he looks exactly like the man who is in the large picture, the only picture, on the front page of the May 12, 1975, issue of the *Black Panther*, the national newspaper created by party founder Huey Newton. It was Fred Bell, the emissary from Texas, the voice from Texas. For the Black Panthers, Texas was like some other country, something beyond even Alabama or anywhere else in the South. Texas was like some inviolable, immutable force, like a beast, really, that was overpowering, bruising, relentless. There were blues songs about the place that seemed to resonate perfectly—"Goin' back to Dallas, take my razor and my gun / . . . There's so much shit in Texas, I'm bound to step in some." When the Black Panthers thought about Texas, they thought about Fred Bell.

"We are going to have to develop a countermilitary entity within our community for self-defense. This is legal, brothers and sisters. We should begin to implement this right now," Fred Bell said then, in the late spring of 1975.

"Today we are gentle. Tomorrow, as the people mobilize, we will be a little less gentle," says Minkah, his voice crackling out of the speakers at the Prince Hall apartments, in the last summer of the 1980s.

On a hot Tuesday in July, somebody came for sixteen-year-old Sheniqua Matthews on Sunnyvale Street. They squeezed the life out of her, ransacked the house, and took the TV and the VCR. A friend of the family found the girl's body near a bedroom.

The very next day, Wednesday, one of Minkah's daughters is on the phone and telling me this: "Daddy's gone to chop down some hedges."

Minkah woke up and went down to the big open killing field off Sunnyvale, close to where Sheniqua Matthews was strangled. I go to see him. If anything, today it looks like there are more rock boys than ever before pea-cocking through the tangled clumps of undergrowth.

Minkah has a chain saw. For the last month he has been coming back to the giant lot at the end of the car wash–crack market. He is, well, garden-ing. Besides the sputtering saw, he has brought tree pruners and hedge clip-pers. The sprawling lot is a thorny ocean of litter and brush, and Minkah is Ishmael, adrift in it. There are an abandoned car, old furniture, waist-high weeds, and a beautiful, fertile-looking pecan tree slowly being choked by a thick, dull-colored vine.

Fahim feverishly cuts the vine where it comes out of the ground. He is sweating, putting his back into it. He is silent, except for some grunting. His muscles strain against his shirt.

Kids smirk as they walk from the East Ledbetter Apartments, through this crack forest, and toward the rock boys at the car wash. For weeks they have watched the middle-aged man come here to chop at the bushes entwined like bundles of snakes. The place still looks out of control.

It looks as if he could be out here forever.

Fahim Minkah continued to align himself with various struggles in Texas—some public, some personal. He was involved in attempts to block a huge NASCAR track from being built inside the city limits of Dallas. He filed a trademark-infringement case against a group in Texas that was using the Black Panther name. And he kept coming back to the crack forest, hacking away at it, trying to seize control of it for almost ten years. By 2000, he had opened a roller-skating rink where the crack forest had once been.

TEXAS HARLEM BLUES

In San Antonio, the Sutton name is legendary, especially on that city's East Side. When I moved to San Antonio, the great liberal politician-lawyer-activist-writer Maury Maverick, Jr.—the words "crusty but benign" were invented for him— took me under his wing. He thought I had some sacred working-class connection to the ghosts of Sacco and Vanzetti. And he said that to even remotely try to understand the unique black world of San Antonio, you had better understand the reach and importance of the Suttons. It seemed like a circle being drawn, some looping back to the beginning. A man from San Antonio, Percy Sutton, was in the heart of the place that Langston Hughes had celebrated, and where Hughes had changed so many things. Sutton became, of course, the proprietor and steward of the most famous building in Harlem, the Apollo Theater. He was a link between Texas and Harlem. We spent a long time together, and he took me on a tour of the inner workings of the Apollo—and he escorted me around Harlem in a nice, long American-made car. He seemed amused, in a good way, at the fact that someone had come from Texas to see him, to write about him, in New York. I never told him—why would I waste his time?—that I had selfish reasons for trying to bridge some things between Texas and New York.

Inching his way west on a positively throbbing 125th Street, maybe the most profound artery in African American history, is supremely slow going for the normally unharnessed Percy Sutton. The Texas man who served as attorney for Malcolm X and his family is taking me on his usual rounds through the soul of Harlem—the zone that, in his own way, he helped define as much as Malcolm, Duke Ellington, Langston Hughes, and so many others did.

The lean man with the hard handshake is aiming for the Apollo Theater, an enduring symbol of American culture and an icon that he also happened to single-handedly dust off and offer to the world.

But every few feet along the supercaffeinated New York City street, someone else wants to beg or boost some sand from the Sutton hourglass. "Mr. Sutton, gotta minute? Can I get your autograph?" inquires a young nurse's aide as she shyly presses her notepad into his hands. A hustling street-corner haberdasher pops out of his place ("Hey, Mr. Harlem," he hollers) to slap Sutton on the back. "Keep fighting for the people," rumbles a guy dressed in foul-smelling rags. A chef says he has come uptown from a fancy downtown restaurant and wants to chow down with Percy Sutton—even if it is at a nearby White Castle hamburger joint.

With every Harlem step taken by the seventy-four-year-old lawyer and kingmaker—he counseled Malcolm X's daughter after she was charged in a plot to assassinate Nation of Islam minister Louis Farrakhan—Sutton follows the path of his own history: He advanced his family's legacy in Texas, and then went on to rewrite the rules of inner-city American politics, right here on 125th Street. He bought media outlets, in Texas and in Harlem, that delivered news and music not being seen or heard at white-owned outlets. He dished out everything from legal advice to political know-how to the Reverend Jesse Jackson, Quincy Jones, and the Kennedy brothers.

He brought Texas to New York City. After the San Antonio native wound his way to the Big Apple following World War II, he set about making Harlem his own. He arguably became its most powerful businessman, owning its most important theater, newspaper, and radio stations. A key civil rights advocate, he lent money and muscle to the Freedom Riders and the NAACP. And he has been an influential, sometimes controversial politician who served as Manhattan borough president—essentially the mayor of Manhattan—for years.

"Percy Sutton is the most extraordinary person I have ever met in my life," insists U.S. representative Charles Rangel (D-NY), who admits that he probably would never have been elected without the Sutton blessing.

"The guy has covered all the damn bases."

If you walk the East Side streets of San Antonio, you are walking with the ghosts of the Sutton family. In San Antonio, a city where African Americans were overshadowed by the larger white and Hispanic communities, Samuel Johnson Sutton and Lillian Viola Smith Sutton were recognized as the leading black couple in town. In a city defined by its proximity to

Mexico, by the sophisticated way its German community linked European tendencies and culture to the frontier, the black neighborhood known as the East Side always labored for a political identity, a voice. In its isolation, literally on the other side of the tracks, a complex, self-defined neighborhood emerged. And the Suttons were the family, in many ways, around which so much revolved. They were farmers, entrepreneurs, philanthropists, and educators—and they also took the time to have fifteen children. Their last child was Percy Ellis Sutton, born November 24, 1920. "I began my first act of communicating by trying to negotiate with all those brothers and sisters," he tells me one day.

His father, a disciplinarian and self-made man who influenced thousands as a longtime school principal, was respected by power brokers as the gatekeeper for votes among South Texas blacks. He also made money in the funeral business—and spent it broadening the minds of his children through books and far-flung travel. Percy Sutton learned a lot about mortality, about the evanescent nature of life—and about the way blacks were treated in both life and death. Blacks, of course, were buried in separate cemeteries. His father had to make his own caskets. His parents would sew the suits and dresses that people wore to their graves. His father was so driven, so intense, that he began to develop a philosophy that he was hell-bent on passing to his children: as black citizens in San Antonio, in Texas, you had to seize control of your destiny or else you would be overtaken by things beyond your control, beyond logic, and beyond the usual dictates of sheer, merciful humanity. You would be consumed, dragged down, if you didn't merge the practical with the spiritual—if you didn't merge cold pragmatism with philanthropy. You had to take care of yourself so you could take care of others. And he drilled that into his children, willing them to be successful, willing them to be strong, to make money, to survive.

"He was absolutely the grand old man of San Antonio. He was Professor Sutton," my friend Maury Maverick, Jr., an ex–state legislator, the son of a former San Antonio mayor, and a direct descendant of Samuel Maverick, tells me one day. He knows everything about San Antonio. "You had to go see the Suttons." Over the decades, there were frequent powerful callers to the Sutton household: key advisers to President Franklin Delano Roosevelt— his so-called Kitchen Cabinet—regularly stayed with the clan, says nephew Chuck Sutton. "I remember picking up the phone when I was a kid, and it was Thurgood Marshall on the other end," adds the nephew.

And meanwhile, Percy Sutton grew up being ordered by his parents to dissect the meaning and use of one new word every day—and to milk four cows every morning, squatting underneath the animals and wearing over-alls on top of his school clothes. Later, he would cruise San Antonio with his father, sitting in the same Studebaker that was used for funeral services, and help distribute the milk to poor people. At age twelve, he pawned a microscope his father had given him (the young man wanted to be a veteri-narian) and hopped trains to New York City, a place his parents had taken him before. For a couple of days he camped out behind a signboard on 155th Street in Harlem—the place he would eventually make his own.

After a short stay, he was back with his parents but still allowing his mind, at least, to wander. Friends remember that the high school principal's son would attach strings to cans and pretend that he was a radio broadcaster: "Good afternoon, ladies and gentlemen, this is Percy Sutton broadcasting from high in the clouds of the Smith-Young Tower . . . ," he would dra-matically announce. Those who knew him say he had lofty goals. "He had real ambitions to be famous," maintains Maverick. Years later, the tin-can dreamer (at other times, he made the imaginary broadcasts with a corncob as a microphone) would purchase his own radio station in San Antonio—and place it atop the Smith-Young Tower.

"It was satisfying," Sutton confesses to me. "I think I bought the station for that reason. It was right across the street from the Alamo, where they wouldn't even allow me to walk on the grass."

There were other episodes when he was "reminded" who he was by peo-ple "saying nigger this and nigger that": not being allowed to walk along the San Antonio River, not being allowed to visit the big bear that he had heard about at the zoo, being told to forget about attending Texas A&M. As a teenager, he learned to fly, then picked up work as a stunt pilot at county fairs. Once while doing a loop, the plane had trouble coming out of a turn. "Take care of me this time and you won't have to worry about me again," the young man said, turning to the heavens. The plane pulled out of the loop. "I checked with him and he was there," laughs Sutton. "I've been in pretty good contact with him since then."

He attended Prairie View A&M and then the Tuskegee Institute—and joined the famous military corps known as the Tuskegee Airmen. During World War II, he was assigned to intelligence-officer training programs in Pennsylvania. In the summer of 1943, before being shipped to Europe, he spent some leave time gambling at The Rhythm Club in Harlem. After he won money, he headed downtown to see the sights around Times Square and 42nd Street. It was a trip that would change his life. There was a woman there in the hot summer of 1943. He just knew she was there. And when he finally spotted her, he liked the way she did the simplest of things: "I met my wife on July 31. It was my destiny. I didn't see her; I felt her presence. I turned around, and there was this gorgeous lady. I watched her a little while, and I liked the way she drank her Coca-Cola."

He asked the woman's companions whether she was married. No, they replied. "I'm going to marry her," he told them. They were wed at the end of November 1943. In December, he was sent to Europe, and he stayed until 1945, serving with the Ninety-ninth Fighter Squadron. Overseas, the intelligence officer was assigned to help defend—even though he wasn't a lawyer—a black soldier accused of raping a woman in Italy. The man was found guilty, but Percy Sutton came to a fateful crossroads. "I decided at that point that I was going to be a lawyer."

When he returned, he also decided to stay away from Texas; like a lot of black soldiers who had been overseas, he decided to move on from his roots and seek his fortune in the big city. Harlem was calling many African Americans. It seemed dizzy with possibilities, the kinds of things that weren't going to be available in East San Antonio. He attended Columbia University Law School and Brooklyn Law School. To pay his way, he worked from four to midnight at the cavernous main U.S. Post Office branch in Manhattan and then from twelve thirty to eight thirty as a subway conductor on the D train. On weekends, he waited tables at Lundy's, a mammoth seafood institution in Brooklyn. "I never believed the system would work for me in Texas," he offers, explaining why he ran so fast in New York. "I'm willing to work long hours, but that was instilled by my parents. I was disciplined to succeed."

The racial hurdles wounded him, though he rarely showed it. "People never really knew the hurt, they knew me as a nice guy. I tell people that it taught me to be angry enough to fight but not so angry as to be bitter," he tells me one day during a rare moment when he has chosen to sit still and reflect. "It is the maintaining of that anger and not doing anything about it that makes you bitter . . . but if you let it out and join causes . . . ," he adds, as I listen to his voice trail off.

From the moment the Texas native settled in New York, he aligned himself with several causes and organizations, especially the NAACP, a group that he would eventually lead in his adopted state. In New York, he pursued his law degree, juggled jobs, and in 1950 was summoned to the Pentagon "to integrate intelligence (units)" during the Korean War. Two and a half years later, he was out of the military again and in possession of his license to practice law. He took a job with an established Harlem lawyer, scrubbing floors and representing clients. At nights, he worked in a token booth in the subway. "I made myself indispensable. I was a lawyer, and I was picking up my own practice. Everywhere I could go, I could get a client. There was a great vitality in Harlem then."

Through the 1950s, and after Sutton opened his own law firm, he began developing a reputation far beyond Harlem's boundaries. Later, he would be a founding member and director of the Reverend Jesse Jackson's PUSH, People United to Save Humanity. He took part in the famous Freedom Rides in the 1960s, attempting to integrate the nation's bus systems. He served on the boards of several organizations, including the Street Literacy Clinic and the Boy Scouts of America. In Texas, in East San Antonio, people were watching the headlines emerge in the black newspapers, the ones that featured Percy Sutton. At several intense levels of the sprawling, dangerous, desegregation movement—strategy sessions, forums, debates, seminars, sit-ins, protests—Sutton was always on hand.

It was hard to figure what was driving him. Some people said you had to understand his roots in Texas. The way he was raised. The way he was raised to analyze, dissect, and deconstruct one new word in the English language every day. The way his father had exposed him to the inconsistencies of life—all those funerals, all those dead bodies he saw as a young man while riding around with his father in funeral entourages. The way his father had raised him: as if his father was the mayor of an unofficial city, as if Sutton was being groomed for something. The police in San Antonio came to the East Side when they had to—not because they really wanted to. That side of town was often just left alone. And if there was a benefit to the neglect, it was that sometimes there was a sense of self-direction; it was as if Percy Sutton grew up in his own version of Harlem in Texas. There were the cultural reference points: Millard McNeal's jazz band, the corner stores, the barbershops, the churches, and the cemeteries. East San Antonio was self-contained—by design, by intent. And Sutton wondered sometimes whether more black Americans should be self-directed, more in charge of their own destiny.

"Nobody has spent more time in the history of the NAACP in keeping it on track. I can think of no one who can go in more states and have more friends," says Rangel, the New York congressman.

Sutton brought a folksy-Texas-meets-intense-Harlem style to his firm, and he built an extensive client base, representing accident victims and people accused of crimes. He began to think about politics through the prism of his legal work—he began to think that he needed to run for office, to speak for people in a public setting. It was, really, what his father had done in San Antonio; his father was, as plenty of people said, the mayor of East San Antonio. "I was specializing in nothing. If you had a trial case, if you had a falling ceiling, if you wanted me to volunteer for some tenants, I would do it. I saw them all as potential voters. I always had serious political interests."

His growing political involvement brought him in contact with Malcolm X at a group debate. It was the bridge to something he felt deep inside. Malcolm knew Sutton in a profound way—he understood him. He understood the connection between Texas and New York. The way things were tied, the way things really weren't that different, the way people coalesced into communities bound by a common language, culture, history—and a common set of bittersweet sorrows. Malcolm knew where Sutton had come from. But as he sized up the hyperkinetic man from East San Antonio, he felt as if he had to press him a bit to see whether he was built for the long haul:

"You know, you do all this talking, but you wouldn't represent a revolutionary," said Malcolm X.

Sutton stared back. "I've represented more revolutionaries than you can actually believe. All those black nationalists out there on 125th Street, they have been my clients and I have not charged them anything. But I do decide who I want to represent."

Malcolm X replied: "Would you represent me?"

Sutton said he would, and at no cost. And he learned to admire Malcolm X's ability to stir people. "He played with words so well. People responded to him. The closest thing that I can remember is when (Nelson) Mandela came here."

Betty Shabazz, Malcolm X's widow, remembers Percy Sutton and his brother—the late New York State Supreme Court judge Oliver Sutton—arriving at her house after her husband was assassinated, in 1965. She had two children, money coming in sporadically, and an uncertain future. The Suttons said they would take care of Malcolm X's family.

"Hey, we're going to help you," said Sutton as he watched Dr. Shabazz's eyes fill with tears. "Why are you crying?"

She replied, "Because you're so kind."

Sutton smiled and said: "No, no, no, you don't understand. This is a business deal."

Years later, Dr. Shabazz laughs at the way Sutton handled the situation. "I know him well enough to say that he is a consummate leader and friend," she tells me. "I consider him a brother, an adviser and a mentor." And when her daughter was named in an alleged murder-for-hire plot to assassinate Farrakhan, she heard from Sutton almost instantly. Without her asking for his help, Sutton immediately took charge of the defense team. Several national headlines later, the charges were set aside. "I told her that I was going to handle it. She didn't have to ask me for help," Sutton says. After pausing for a second, he laughs. "My guess is that it worked out quite well."

Dr. Shabazz tells me she considers herself part of Percy Sutton's extended family.

"And there are a lot of Suttons," she says.

His burgeoning political interests led him to run for office in New York. He was elected to the New York State Assembly in 1964. Two years later, he took over as Manhattan borough president and stayed in the position until 1977. That year, he lost a Democratic primary bid to become the first black mayor of New York. His friends say that loss was one that hit home, especially after years spent building a broad base of support. "To see that support crumble was a terrible disappointment, to see how fragile those friendships were," says Rangel.

In 1972, Sutton had founded the Inner City Broadcasting Corporation, a sprawling multimedia firm that would branch into radio stations, cable outlets, and television production—and an enterprise that he would later turn over to several younger Suttons. In 1980, he paid $220,000 to rescue the boarded-up Apollo Theater from bankruptcy. He set about restoring the theater and bringing to life the fallen symbol of the Harlem Renaissance. The Apollo is one of the most famous theaters in the world, home to countless legendary performances by the leading African American artists of the time: Billie Holiday, James Brown, Ella Fitzgerald, and on and on. It was, for many, the most potent, vibrant symbol of African American artistic contributions. Sutton knew, from his days growing up in San Antonio, the meaning of symbolism—the way buildings, blocks, neighborhoods can symbolize something beyond the obvious. Hell, he grew up within walking distance of the Alamo, but he wasn't allowed to walk on the grass.

Harlem experienced a resurgence; some said it was good, some said it was a regrettable change. There was massive gentrification, capped off, perhaps, by former president Bill Clinton deciding to open his offices on 125th Street, not far from the Apollo. As the beautiful old brownstone buildings began going on the market for millions, they were scooped up by white residents attracted by new restaurants and stores. The most famous black neighborhood in America was changing in ways that almost no one could have predicted. Many people said it all stemmed from Percy Sutton's restoring the one building around which the community had coalesced—the most famous building, ever, in Harlem.

When Percy Sutton was young, his father spelled out part of his philosophy: "You ought to try and own everything, but you will make money by helping people, by doing the right thing." For a while, he owned the *Amsterdam News*, one of the most influential inner-city papers serving black readers. And for New Yorkers who listened to WLIB (the first black-owned radio station in New York City) and WBLS, he featured music and shows on black-themed issues that no one else would touch.

Beginning in the 1980s, as he neared the end of his career, he began to gently relinquish control, turning over parts of his media empire to his family. His son Pierre succeeded him as chairman of Inner City; his daughter Cheryl held a variety of executive positions within the Sutton business group; one nephew ran radio stations in San Antonio. "I personally saw Percy Sutton do something that was very, very hard for a father to. He has been able to stand apart," says nephew Charles Andrews. "Percy Sutton is a man who very much believes in family. He has done many things over his life, but he has never, ever, failed to give family members an opportunity to go along with him."

Well into the 1990s, he remained a fixture in Harlem and slipped into that stage of life where earnest young people came to visit him—there were hagiographies, oral histories. He lived on 135th Street in a modest Harlem apartment building. Although he easily could have afforded to, he refused to leave Harlem for pricier digs in expensive neighborhoods. It was as if he were hanging on to what he remembered about East San Antonio, and when he first made the trip to Harlem. As if he were still remembering the way African Americans in Texas and Harlem were bound by the same bits of fate and circumstance, the same swirl of history.

He tells me he can still see himself as a young man in Texas. He can still see the tall buildings on the other side of the tracks in San Antonio. He can still see the beauty, the merit, in being exiled and being forced to build your own city . . . the way his father had done it, the way he had envisioned it in Harlem. He says that he talks to young people and says this: "You see this bald-headed old man who is speaking to you? Do me a favor. At the height of your success, when you are seated at the positions of power, walking the corridors of consequence, please don't forget who you are . . . where you have come from . . . or those who shook the apple trees of power and brought those apples down.

"Think about them, and then reach back and bring someone else across."

Percy Sutton remained affiliated with various political and civil rights issues. For years, he accepted awards and talked, in various interviews, about the things that bound him to both Texas and the black mecca also known as Harlem.

PART TWO
COMMUNITY

CONGO STREET BLUES

One of my friends was a good-hearted photographer named Randy Eli Grothe, someone who knew music very well. We traveled a lot together—to see Hopi elders in Arizona, to see bluesmen in the Delta, to travel with Sandinista soldiers fighting the contras in remote parts of northern Nicaragua, to watch American missionaries try to convert communists in Red Square. Music was a tie that bound us. In Moscow, we gave away Texas blues tapes to musicians we met. In a grocery store on the Navajo nation, we bought cassette tapes of peyote chants, prayers, and war songs. In Dallas, we would drive around in search of the blues. Long lunches, "taking the pulse of the city," in case editors asked. We were usually in pawnshops, going down alleys, looking for something.

We passed by Congo Street and agreed that we should linger there. We talked about moving into a house on the block, maybe renting a small bungalow and just moving in. That seemed contrived, more contrived than usual. So we parked our car at one end of the street and walked, like clever versions of Mormon missionaries, from one end of the street to the other. Day after day. For a few weeks. We went at night, to see how the sun set. We tried to be there early in the morning, before anyone left home. We were there when the school buses unloaded the kids. We went to side streets and mom-and-pop businesses. We were always, it seemed, on parade, as if we were walking along a submerged esplanade—the stoops sat so high that anyone on them was looking down at us. It was hard, every day, to explain our objectifying premise. We were there for one reason, one word, only: Congo.

The same strange stare came all morning, the day when a little piece of Texas history had its annual resurrection. Alleys and lawns in the neighborhoods unfurling from Fair Park in Dallas had been cleared. Room was being made for the cars carrying visitors to the big Texas-Oklahoma football game in the Cotton Bowl.

On the street Ronnie Young grew up on, people were pushing hard to lure those customers to parking spots on the grass and alongside homes. But Young—everyone calls him Hop because polio left him with a limp—was flying. He lifted a fallen tree, by himself, from in front of the empty house at the west end of the block. Then he ran toward traffic and began waving his arms, steering his first car toward the small patch of earth. When the football fans popped out of an Oldsmobile with Oklahoma license plates, they pressed some cash into Hop's hand and then stopped and gave that quick, queer stare.

They were looking at the sign over Hop's head: Congo Street.

The name Congo is enough to bring most strangers to a halt. And any familiarity with Texas's racial history has to summon questions about Congo. About its history. About who lives there. But people, like me, looking for answers, the ones who turn down Congo, simply find more questions. Congo isn't like anything else. It is the thinnest of blocks, a small slice in the lower half of East Dallas. Bottle-shaped, one quarter of it is barely wide enough for one car. The rest is a tight squeeze for two. There are no sidewalks. You enter it as if there are invisible gates at either end. If you come by foot, you are on display in the middle of the corridor. Porches push close to the curb. When I walk down Congo, people follow me from behind wooden screen doors.

Those people whose eyes trail my back will tell you that there were, still are, times when those who lived on Congo felt as if they were the ones on display. As if they had been assigned there, steered toward Congo by the confining, inflexible patterns that governed all of Texas. Maybe it was those unwritten laws, but today Congo seems lifted from another era. Congo looks and feels insular, as insular as any small town.

"This is where blacks had to stay," says Sammie Clayton, sitting on her mother's front porch on Congo and carefully watching me. The more she thinks about Congo, and the thousand different things it implies, the angrier she gets. She challenges me: "They didn't name any other block 'Congo,' did they?"

They didn't. City records show that Congo Street was an alley in the early 1920s. In 1924, the alley was designated Carroll Drive, to distinguish it from the street it intersected, Carroll Avenue. The alley was described as "all colored." In 1933, Carroll Drive became Congo Street. The people in the city records office don't know why. Sammie Clayton does. From her porch, she carefully watches cars pulling into the available spots. Her brother, daughter, grandson, and some friends are sitting with her. Mrs. Clayton's eyes are wide open.

"It don't take a damn genius to figure it out," she shouts at me.

On Congo, the street closes in on you, and it is as if you can hear everything on the block—and everyone can hear you. The houses are close to one another, so close you can almost stand between two, stretch your arms, and touch each one. Sammie Clayton's relatives grow quiet and look away from her, from me.

"Blacks were sent down the alley," yells Mrs. Clayton. "We were sent to Congo."

Sent somewhere. Dispatched, steered, exiled, and the name of the street was changed. One day, just like that, a sign went up, and the alley became permanently known as Congo. And people who lived there knew their street was different. It looked different; it felt different. People had been left there.

Sent to Congo.

The matriarch of Congo Street, ninety-two-year-old Pauline Lillia Williams, is settled on her old spongy couch, her face full of the ghostly glow from a television. She is counting the money she made that morning by helping park cars for the football game. Earlier in the day, she had hauled out a rusting metal chair, a plastic Pepsi bottle filled with water, and some rolled-up papers to use as a fan. While she sat under a solitary gnarled mesquite tree, her great-grandson Pookie, waving a red rag tied to a stick, lured customers into the carefully mowed empty lot alongside Pauline's house.

All day Miss Pauline—the daughter of Perilla and Levi Davis of Palestine, Texas, is called Miss Pauline by everyone on the block—filled her worn black purse with five-dollar bills. Down the block, Carl was asking four dollars a car. But Carl, guiding cars with an empty, bright red STP container, was using a lot that sparkled with mounds of broken glass. Miss Pauline wasn't having any of that. She kept her lot clean. She wanted five dollars.

While Miss Pauline counts her money, Opal Jackson moves inside a house a few feet across the ribbon of street. The people on Congo call Mrs. Jackson, who is sixty-four, "the midget lady." Her short legs unnaturally curl when she sits down. When darkness comes and Mrs. Jackson goes to answer my knock at her door, she casts a huge shadow on her cream-colored walls. But when she arrives at the battered front screen, her sweat-covered forehead barely reaches above the first cross panel. Mrs. Jackson is cooking vinegar and lemon pies, using old recipes from the white-owned farm her family grew up on in Forney. And she is waiting for fireworks to paint the sky over Fair Park.

"I couldn't work in the fields like all the rest of the children," says Mrs. Jackson. "So I learned how to sew and cook. I was the one who had to take care of all the babies. When everyone was out working, I cared for twenty-eight babies. I had to cook for all of them too."

Mrs. Jackson still sews. She never uses a pattern. She sees something she likes and she makes it. Outdoors, in the dusk, she falls back into her rusted metal chair and watches people walking by.

"My husband died on Congo Street," the midget lady says, as she raises a hand. "Right there." She's pointing me toward a spot a few feet away, a few feet off the curb.

Her husband Tom was playing ball with the kids on the block. It was 1972. There were dozens of kids jammed into the street, several from each of the twenty-four wooden shotgun homes. Tom, diabetic, keeled over in the middle of the game.

"He had bad sugar," offers Mrs. Jackson, looking away from me and rocking back and forth.

The fireworks at the nearby state fair should be coming soon. There is a sense, on Congo, that you are on a train that is idling at the base of a mountain and that you are looking up and out through vaguely smeared windows. Things happen on the other side of the glass, they are etched in the sky. Noise comes from over the mesquite trees. From somewhere over there, out there.

Mrs. Jackson watches the Hunt children, Lorenzo and Derrick, toss a football between the parked cars. "We never had no children. I guess I must have wanted them too bad. I used up all my energy wanting them."

Night is coming. Mrs. Jackson never wants to leave Congo. "I can't drive a car, so I like it here. I'm close to everything." When she needs to take a trip, she calls a cab. "Sometimes when I call one, I have to spell it out to them. C-o-n-g-o," the midget lady tells me. "Sometimes it seems like a lot of people don't want to find it. Well, we're still here."

People in the city's records office speculate that Congo Street might have come into being because of the upcoming Texas Centennial extravaganza at the State Fair, in 1936. Because Dallas was bracing for a swarm of visitors. But what kind of message was Dallas sending out when Carroll Drive was changed to Congo Street?

"Dallas is always doing strange things with its street names," says Texas historian A. C. Greene. He wonders whether a city planner, in a moment of whimsy, named it after Vachel Lindsay's 1914 poem "The Congo":

THEN I SAW THE CONGO, CREEPING THROUGH THE BLACK
CUTTING THROUGH THE JUNGLE WITH A GOLDEN TRACK.

City councilman Al Lipscomb, who grew up a few blocks from Congo, tells me he sees malice instead of rhyme. Any message sent out from the name change was poisoned. "It was a cruel, bad joke. They were trying to let people know that this was Nigger Town. Sure, the Texas Centennial was coming. And they were trying to let people know where Nigger Town was."

Congo was once at the heart of one of the solitary outposts for blacks in East Dallas. John McKenzie—Miss Pauline's son, nicknamed Peanut—recites the boundaries of the small zone: "There was West Street, Bank Street, Carroll Avenue, and Parry. And Congo was right in the middle. This was the place where everyone congregated. Blacks weren't supposed to go anywhere else. Congo was kind of where you had to be."

Some people have never left. Fourteen of the twenty-four houses on Congo are occupied. Everyone in those homes can tell you the names of every other person on the block. People have lived here for years: Opal Jackson for almost thirty, Ernest Garrett for fifteen, Lily Jackson for twenty, Elbert Carter for more than twenty. Miss Pauline for almost sixty. And most of the people on Congo are related to one another. Elbert Carter's mother-in-law lives across the street. Annie Pearl Garrett's daughter Vanessa lives next door. Vanessa's brother Ernest lives next door to her. Elbert's stepfather runs Kenneth's Barber Shop, around the corner. Scooter Carter is a cousin of Jesse James Jackson's son Richard. All the kids on the block seem to be cousins.

Years ago there were even more nearby relatives, grocery stores, and things that anchored the place in time. Many of the businesses were Italian, just as they were in black neighborhoods all over the South. It was that way years ago on Thomas Street in Dallas's large, pivotal black neighborhood just north of downtown, the neighborhood called North Dallas before that name became synonymous with the myth and reality of Dallas's push toward Oklahoma. It was that way on Lyons Avenue in Houston's Fifth Ward and at the intersection of Issaquena and Fourth streets in Clarksdale, Mississippi.

Near Congo, Carlo and Constantina Angelo were running a grocery and butcher shop in a rambling plank building. The LaBarba family had a store around the corner. Elbert Carter once went to work for Carlo and learned how to make Italian sausage. Carlo came to Carter's wedding, where fifty people jammed into a house on Congo. And Miss Pauline cared for Carlo's son; sometimes she would cut a switch from a Congo Street tree to keep him in line.

Today, most of the businesses—except for Sal and Tony's liquor store—are gone or changed. Iranian immigrants run Carlo's store. Different families have drifted onto and off the block. A few years ago there were several unwelcome neighbors. People who let their yards get away from them. People who had loud visitors. Those outsiders finally left, but so did some of the relatives, the friends who moved to bigger homes in Pleasant Grove and South Dallas. It was self-contained again, but seemed even smaller.

"I sure hope they keep this little street," says Elbert Carter, who is now a truck driver for Lone Star Gas. Like everyone else on the block, he wrestles with what he is familiar with and what he doesn't know. And he learned long ago to not run away from what Congo means, implies. "My friends in Oak Cliff tell me I should move off Congo. I like it here."

Down the block, Peanut is pacing back and forth in front of his mother's house. "Now, listen to me," he says. "We used to call this street The Island. The older dudes still call it The Island. When you get on Congo, you get stuck. I know that much."

Peanut made his move to Oak Cliff a few years ago. But, every day, you will find him back on Congo Street, sometimes perched on a porch. The porches on Congo sit way up high. They are made for waiting and watching. They are the same porches you see on the streets back behind Louis Armstrong Park in New Orleans. On the streets curling away from the railroad tracks in Leland, Mississippi. On the streets across from Ernest Hemingway's old home in Key West, Florida. They are southern versions of the brownstone stoops in East New York, twin sisters of the porches in Houston's Fourth Ward. They are the train seats on a train that doesn't move.

In the afternoons, an hour after the school bus lets kids off, a city bus deposits "Mama" Liz Plant and Lily Mae Jackson near Grand Avenue. They both work as maids in North Dallas. So does Vivian Carter. Miss Pauline used to cook for white families who lived on fancy South Boulevard in South Dallas. Even at the age of ninety-two, she talks about wanting to go back to work.

After they exit the city bus, Mrs. Plant and Mrs. Jackson walk past the Fair Park Church of God in Christ and the empty patch of land on the west end and hook a turn down Congo Street. The first house they pass is Miss Pauline's. When the old grocery store went out of business a few years ago, and when Carlo and the other Italians who had run stores left the neighborhood, Miss Pauline began selling candy and soda water out of her house. The Mexican American families who live across Carroll Avenue say her prices are cheap.

Before the sun sets, Mrs. Plant and Mrs. Jackson have taken their positions on Mrs. Plant's porch. They look like sentinels at the Bank Street end of Congo. Mrs. Plant sits in her chair with her back to the front door. Mrs. Jackson leans against one of the two wood columns as she holds up the afternoon paper. Today, the women are stony and suspicious. Mrs. Jackson's face is also proud and unforgiving. They are the oral historians, the keepers. They want to know what I am doing on their block. They don't want liberal white anthropologists; they don't want to be studied, singled out. They know what Congo Street is. It's just a street. A small street that you can go by and not even notice.

"People have been wondering what you are doing on this block," says Mrs. Jackson.

Mrs. Plant nods: "We don't like strangers on our block. What we need are people who are going to put meat on our table."

I don't know what to tell them, other than to tell them that they are right, of course. And I tell them that I just wanted to know what life was like on a street named Congo. It makes no sense, obviously, and we all look in different directions. *It is just a street*, a little block buried in a big city in Texas. And sometimes, when it is hot, there are the ubiquitous heat waves, and things feel distorted and unfocused, and everything seems to be a shade of gray . . . all the colors flushed away, like the pages of an old book soaking in a puddle. It could be any decade, any time, out here. It could be 1929. It could be 1959. Congo Street looks sealed in, as if we are standing on a block built inside a bottle. The street is tapered at either end, and it is as if something is hovering overhead, looking down at this artifice, this place. It is probably time to go home—for everyone to go back indoors, back to their cars. Some people are convinced there are ghosts on the street. Maybe it is time for them to come out.

The weak streetlights, soupy globes hanging over the tangles of wires that bind both sides of the block, are still warming up. The Garrett family's gray rabbit is making a break for the weed-filled shortcut to East Grand Avenue, taking a look behind before being swallowed by the blanket of darkness spread under Elbert Carter's black Cadillac. From the west, a swell of cackles and mechanical noises reaches the street. The jumble of screams and excited sounds retreats into the dim halo above Fair Park. It is the first day of the

State Fair of Texas—and Carter's wife, Vivian, swears that on still evenings, when the distant din subsides for a second, you can hear the disembodied voice of Big Tex echoing up and down the thin block.

There are things on Congo Street, things that people can't name or clearly see but that they are sure are real. Congo Street has its past, and it has its shadows.

Mrs. Carter, sitting on her front porch, has just finished telling me about one particular ghost that lives on Congo Street. Big Daddy—his real name was Seymour—lived directly across from the Carters. A few years ago, Big Daddy passed away inside his falling-down house. The Carters found Big Daddy as he was dying. Elbert Carter held him in his arms.

"He never did talk to me. And then, when I was holding him, he kept trying to tell me something," says Carter. He listened hard, but Elbert couldn't understand what Big Daddy was trying to say.

After Big Daddy died, his ghost moved into 4522 Congo. At night, you can see a light in there. Sometimes Carter smells coffee coming from the house. "I don't drink coffee," he offers to me.

Mrs. Carter is staring at her husband. They were married twenty-three years ago, in the house next door to Big Daddy's. They have a dozen different relatives living on Congo Street.

"You think we're lying, don't you?" Mrs. Carter asks me.

She has more ghost stories. "You don't know the half of it. When we first moved into this house, blood used to come up through the floor."

Her husband shakes his head.

I am watching them, and they know I am listening, writing things down. They know I don't belong. A few weeks ago, I had thought about moving onto Congo, moving into one of the bungalows for rent at the end of the block. In schools, people talk about "immersion" writing, "immersion sociology." It is an admirable but dangerous conceit. Dangerous because it sometimes seems like the overtly right thing to do, but it can be tainted by paternalism, by pious missteps, by an urban colonialism that can never be surmounted.

It is getting dark on Congo Street.

"Congo is like a little town. There's a lot of things about Congo . . ." begins Carter.

His wife cuts him off.

"Forget it," she says.

"It's just a street where a bunch of people live."

Congo Street still exists. City planners are vague about its future. One leading black historian thinks that Congo Street will eventually be erased so that there will be easier routes between Fair Park and other parts of the city, county, and state. Someone noted this a long time ago: when people in the area look toward the largest Ferris wheel in North America, at Fair Park, they can see that—from their perspective—the word "Texas" is spelled backward on that amusement-park ride.

FREE MAN BLUES

Inside cities, there are certain zones that seem to be almost clinically, neatly set off from everything else. The usual flow or evolution from one neighborhood to another isn't there. Joppa was that way, and because it was so isolated, you would go there only if you had to. You didn't necessarily pass through it on the way to somewhere else. It was across the tracks, settled in the woods, set apart. Like so many things on the southern side of Dallas, it seemed, at times, never to have existed. County commissioner John Wiley Price told me that there were two areas in Dallas that needed to be written about: Joppa and a place called Sand Branch. And Dallas being what it is—a place with many things hidden—sometimes that frisson of expectation, of discovery, gets ramped up just as your car bumps over the railroad tracks. Coming into Joppa, which is part of Dallas, was almost like entering a self-contained small town in the Deep South. Complete with the elders, the oral historians, who knew exactly why Joppa was there . . . and who knew exactly why God's dream had been deferred. Some people seemed tired, disbelieving, when I knocked on their doors. I sat in church on a Sunday and wondered what unholy thing I had embarked on. I was a stranger in the sanctuary, in the back row this time, and what was I writing down? Truth be told, I was looking for a metaphor, I was looking for something symbolic in the sermon. Something I could use in my story. Reporters know to do this at disasters. They go to churches in the wake of hurricanes, tornadoes, plane crashes, school-bus crashes . . . and they wait for the preacher to read the right Bible passage, to say the thing that will make the story poignant. In Joppa, going to the church was probably redundant. The metaphors were everywhere. They were already, literally, in the damned Bible.

He saw in a vision . . . an angel of God coming . . .
    And when he looked on him, he was afraid, and said, What is it,
Lord? And he said unto him, Thy prayers and thine alms are come up for
a memorial before God.
    And now send men to Joppa.

—ACTS 10:3–5

All through the dark Tuesday morning, police cars are bumping down Charlie Jackson's block, kicking up the caked country earth, thudding over the land that holds so many secrets, the first land that the first Dallas freedmen called their own.

The police are out again. And though she doesn't want to believe it— though she tries to shut the thought out of her head—Charlie Jackson knows why they are here. No need to peek out the window of her small house or send one of her young sons to investigate.

There is a body.

Someone has come to Joppa—a part of the city that is still like part of the country, a hidden neighborhood with eighteen streets and eighteen churches—and dumped a body. Someone has sought out this piece of Texas—isolated, sealed off by the river, the railroad tracks, and two highways—and used it to bury dirty secrets. And now there again is blood in the ghostly woods that blanket Joppa, one of the country's historic African American freedmen's towns. And there are painful echoes in clusters of oak and pecan trees around Honey Springs, the curl of water that soothed the throats of those first freed slaves. Echoes in the place where the Ku Klux Klan once had its torture grounds. Where, until the late 1970s, some people were still collecting rainwater to drink. Where a community blossomed at the foot of an old slave plantation and now shares an edgy border with a grand country club that would like to see Joppa go away.

Charlie Jackson has lived half a century in this old freedmen's village. She has heard the stories, and, like the elders who live around her, she still hears those echoes. And now Charlie Jackson knows, deep inside her heart, that it is as if nothing has really ever changed in the town that time forgot.

In the biblical city of Joppa—the seaport for ancient Jerusalem and a place whose name, according to local preachers, can be translated as "beautiful" or "the beginning"—Peter was praying on a rooftop. He was hungry, engulfed in self-doubt and wrestling with the question of who was truly allotted a place in God's kingdom. He had a vision in which the heavens opened and a vessel descended. On it were four-legged animals, winged creatures, and crawling beasts. A voice rang out: "Rise, Peter, kill and eat."

Peter said that he couldn't, that he had never eaten anything unclean or common.

The voice boomed back: "What God has cleansed, that you will not call common."

Three times, Peter heard the message. When he awoke, he had no idea what it meant. The next day, he traveled from Joppa to a nearby city, where the people fell on their knees before him. Suddenly, Peter's vision became clear: "Stand up, I myself also am a man," he told them. "God has shown me that I should not call any man common or unclean."

The people who settled in the south-central part of Dallas in the late 1800s and who gave it the name Joppa also had a vision of a world where no man would be considered common or unclean. They knew that God had cleansed every man. Along the gurgling Honey Springs, in that part of Dallas that was at once both Beautiful and The Beginning, freed slaves from the old Miller plantation began to clear bois d'arc and oak trees. They knew, as people have always known in Texas, that true wealth is the land. After the Juneteenth emancipation of slaves in Texas, several freedmen's towns emerged as former slaves settled onto land of their own. Joppa, south of the Trinity and east of the old road to Austin, was one of the first.

And because of where it was—because of its natural and man-made boundaries—Joppa was destined to be different. "They had to hide, they had to get away from the white community," Larry Duncan, a local politician, once told me. "They are an island; they are isolated. There was a time, as a freedmen's community, when they needed those barriers."

The erudite Donald Payton, one of the leading African American historians in Dallas, has spent years researching the evolution of Joppa. His ancestors, slaves on the Miller plantation, were some of the freedmen who first settled the community. He tells me the story: Joppa was founded by Henry Critz Hines, a slave who had been shipped to the Miller plantation from Missouri. He was forwarded as a piece of property that needed protection until the end of the Civil War. As soon as the war was over, his master planned to send for his property. But after emancipation, Henry Hines refused to go back to Missouri. By the 1870s, he owned and ran a crucial ferry across the Trinity, one of the few ways to get across the unpredictable, untamed river.

What was even more stunning than a freed slave so quickly commanding one of the most important avenues of Texas commerce was the fact that Henry Hines's extended family began to carve out its own community—

its own city—not far from the Miller plantation. They called it Joppa, or sometimes Joppee, Joppie, and even Jaffe. By the turn of the century, small cabins had gone up. By the early 1900s, they had been replaced by shotgun shacks, wooden bungalows, and prairie cottages with plenty of room for porches. Many of the families that joined the Hines settlers were country people escaping the racist tendencies of old East Texas towns, places where the Ku Klux Klan would run especially strong and deep in the 1920s. They came to Joppa to be close to Dallas, but not inside it; they wanted the progressiveness of the city but some semblance of a bond with Mother Earth.

"It was quiet. I could lay out in my yard," Gracie Burrell, ninety-four, whose grandmother was a slave, tells me.

Miss Burrell, born in 1899, slowly talks about her early life in East Texas and the things that brought her to Joppa in the 1930s: "White people kept us when I was growing up. It wasn't nothing for a man to be beat to death. A lot of people just didn't know any better."

Through the 1940s and 1950s, Joppa's homesteaders from all around Texas were joined by families leaving South Dallas, the freedmen's town in old North Dallas, and the Trinity River bottomlands—places where blacks had been exiled into housing projects and old homes turned into apartments after World War II. In Joppa, the Crowders, the Highs, the Miles, the Blairs, the Kings, and the other families could own a plot of land, maybe a half acre. They could have chickens, rabbits, even a cow. The greens grew so high that children could disappear inside them. The well water was bracing, cool, and there were swimming spots where Honey Springs turned a corner and carved out deep holes. It was, remember the people who migrated there, humble but pristine. It was also something else. It was south. South when the twentieth-century land speculators, the men who envisioned Dallas as a glittering Oz on the prairie, were relentlessly looking north.

That drive north spelled the end for many other freedmen's towns, most visibly the one called North Dallas or, sometimes, the State-Thomas neighborhood. Highways ripped through the community just north of the Woodall Rodgers Freeway. Midnight creepers came with gas cans and torches and destroyed community landmarks such as Page's Temple. Finally, the city neglected the neighborhood until homes were condemned, destroyed, or bought up by real estate speculators. But Joppa, on the outskirts of town, was protected. Protected by being to the south, protected by its isolation. Protected, in the end, by the very things that would conspire to keep it neglected.

The old South Central Expressway cut it off on the west, along with the sprawling Southern Pacific railroad yards. The Trinity River sealed Joppa on the north. A private country club became a complete firewall to the east. Loop 12 was the barrier to the south, along with landfills, garbage dumps, and gravel pits that still pockmark the area. Even though it was incorporated into a growing Dallas in the 1950s, Joppa seemed locked into a world of unpaved streets, hand pumps, outhouses, and rain barrels. There was a community horse named Dan, a café called The Holiday Inn, and honky-tonks called Cat on the Roof, the Pleasure Garden, and The Red Top, where Big Bo Thomas and the Twistin' Arrows would play and Dallas musical legends like R. L. Griffin would join in on drums. For years, only one of its eighteen streets could take you in or out of Joppa. And when the railroad ran, as it still does today, that street was closed. No way out and no way in for police, ambulance drivers, firefighters, sanitation workers, or clean-up crews. Come death, birth, hell, or even the high fetid waters of the Trinity, Joppa was cut off from Dallas—and from the rest of Texas.

At Laurabelle Foster's house, the walls seem to dip down to listen as her voice slips to a whisper. She is telling me about the dangerous work she embarked upon in the 1940s, the first work of organizing Joppa. Organizing at a time when the Klan was all too near. She presses a thin hand to her bony face, and her eighty-seven-year-old body seems to coil. In her other hand, her fingers are curling tightly around the business end of an old thick cane.

Sixty to seventy years ago—and five hundred yards northeast of Joppa's New Zion Baptist Church—the Dallas Klan actively maintained its whipping posts, trees whose lower limbs had been cleared away so that a man could be bound to a trunk. Newspaper accounts included interviews with people who had been spirited away from their inner-city Dallas homes and taken out to Joppa. "You're not so bad off," F. H. Etheredge, an East Dallas lumberman, was told as he was being handcuffed to the tree in 1922. "Sixty-three other men have been whipped in the last few months."

And when reporters fanned out into Joppa, they recorded the words of the freedmen's families who were living in Beautiful and The Beginning: "We usually go to bed early. When dark comes, I take my family in the house and shut the doors . . . and I don't go out very often. We often hear a lot of automobiles going by and hear people talking and some of them yelling, but we don't pay any attention to them . . . We attend to our own business. That's their business. I'm not going to tell anything because I don't know anything to tell."

Years later, Joppa's elders, the ones who protect the secret knowledge, stare hard at strangers like me who come into their seventy-year-old homes and ask questions about those torture grounds. About those times when the strange automobiles would come scraping over the country roads, about those voices echoing in the night from deep inside the woods of Joppa. Some of them, such as eighty-six-year-old Arelia Watson, fix me with a hard stare: "No comment."

Some of them, such as Laurabelle Foster, will shake their heads and slowly, slowly tell me about their trials: "God wasn't going to let them bother me," hisses Miss Laurabelle, born in the country woods outside of Athens, Texas, and mother of Charles and Howard Jean. "Yeah, they'd come up here. We just went on and prayed."

Prayed that the dangerous thing she was embarking upon would work. In the 1940s, Foster thought she and others should organize their homeland. So she borrowed chairs from Blair's Temple and called a house meeting. People whispered to her: "You're fixing to cause trouble. Wait and see."

She persisted: "I knew nothing in the world about organizations," she remembers as she stares out her old screen door. Sitting in her rocker, she slides her feet across the weathered hardwood floors of the house her late husband built fifty years ago. "But they just didn't want to give us anything."

So across those same hardwood floors, years ago, she paced back and forth, outlining what she wanted, what she hoped everyone in Beautiful and The Beginning would also want: Lights. Water. Paved streets. Sewer service. Garbage pickup. All the things that other parts of Dallas had. Laurabelle Foster called her group the South Central Civic League. And today, as she quietly sits in her small house with the faded white walls, she occasionally thinks of the battles, the sleepless nights, the bitterness. Waiting, ignored, at old city hall on Harwood Street. Waiting from sunrise to sunset and finally watching as the lights went out and the doors were locked. Praying, hoping, the preachers in Dallas would help—and learning that "they didn't have time for us folks out here."

And sometimes Laurabelle Foster thinks about her neighbors in Joppa, the ones who scoop up the fallen pecans, who carve away at the forests of trumpet vines, and who stab their canes at the ground as they walk the narrow lanes. She thinks about the ones who were the sons, daughters, and grandchildren of freed slaves. The ones who had never owned anything before and who came to realize that their property was better off left hidden. And that they were better off being quiet, turning away from those echoes in the woods . . . attending to their own business . . . not telling anything because they didn't know anything to tell.

It is the silence that still lures the strangers. Strangers who don't see Joppa as either Beautiful or The Beginning. Strangers who probably haven't read about Joppa in the Bible. Strangers who, as the Ku Klux Klan once did, use Joppa as a place for torturing the living and dumping the dead.

And into the 1990s, Charlie Jackson was right. Nothing changed. That Tuesday morning, two men had tied up Michael Lee Jackson, put him in the trunk of a car, and headed for Joppa. Once in the woods, they shot the twenty-eight-year-old man in the head, back, and shoulder and left him for dead. Somehow, Michael Lee Jackson survived. He crawled to a house on Yancy Street, the same street that Charlie Jackson lives on. Calls were made, he went to the hospital, the police began their investigation, and Charlie—a woman with a wide, open face and glasses occasionally perched on the end of her nose—decided that enough was enough.

She had grown up in Joppa and knew everyone on those eighteen streets. And though she is a licensed vocational nurse, Jackson was more the mayor of Joppa than anything else. Her life became consumed by a million questions: Why couldn't Joppa be Beautiful or The Beginning again? How could Joppa escape being swallowed whole?

The day after the man was dumped down the block, she decided to call another community meeting—she had been holding them for years, just as Laurabelle Foster once did. Now, all week, Charlie sent out her troops— her children, all the neighborhood children, her friend Denise Fowler— armed with fliers announcing an important meeting. The fliers went into the wooden mailbox at the Montgomery house, where Old Man Montgomery still kicks up an occasional tombstone when he puts in his garden. It was just after World War II that the Montgomerys settled there, and they still remember when, soon after moving day, a 100-year-old man told them that the house was built on top of a nineteenth-century cemetery.

The fliers went into the hands of the parents busy signing their children up for grade school in Wilmer-Hutchins. Parents like Marvin Burrell: "The people in the community try to nurture the kids along. I don't know if a lot of communities that are in the lower-to-middle-income level are like that." He tells me there has always been a sense of family, of watching out for youngsters. "When we were coming up, Mrs. So-and-so would always have permission to whip my behind."

The fliers went into the door slots of the three businesses in Joppa: Early Gibson's Laundromat, the thinly stocked candy store, and burly Reverend Leonard Skyler's barbershop. The fliers went into the hands of people waiting for the bus to go downtown, to go anywhere, since there are no jobs in Joppa. And up the fliers went into the mail slot for New Zion Baptist Church, a place where the Reverend B. F. Brown still likes to go into the aisles on Sundays and caress his congregation with sweet thunder: "Ask if you have hellhounds on your trail, ask if you need understanding, ask if you need peace, ask if you need a friend. Have you tried him, early in the morning? Do you believe that the streets are paved with gold?"

The Tuesday-evening meeting is called to order in the Gethsemane Baptist Church, another of the eighteen churches that go along with those eighteen streets in Joppa. On this achingly hot and still August night, Charlie steps to the front of the old house of worship. Forty of Joppa's 700 or so residents are sitting quietly in the pews. With the ceiling fans barely slicing the humid air and the occasional latecomer arriving in overalls, it looks—it feels—like Deep East Texas instead of a neighborhood in America's seventh-largest city.

"I know you are familiar with the trash, the furniture, cars, and now . . . bodies being left for dead," Charlie begins in her matter-of-fact voice. In the hard-backed pews, old men lean forward, struggling to hear her words. Old women wave paper fans. It could be 1893, the year that nearby New Zion became the first church in Joppa to open its doors. All forty of these people live in Joppa, and all forty know the names of everyone in the room.

"This is our home," Charlie goes on.

One or two voices from the pews urge her on, urge her to push ahead with the message. These are people who say they love living in Joppa. Who say that, yes, it is poor, but that it is still a place with tall oak trees, a meandering creek, children who run in the street.

Denise Fowler is one of the many at the meeting who has lived in Joppa since she was a baby. "If I won the lottery today, I would still stay out here," she explains to me. "I'll probably be out here until the day I die. I chose to live here. We're not just going to give our property away. If we stay together, it will be OK. We want more attention than just every Juneteenth—maybe the other 364 days a year," the thirty-two-year-old says. Not long ago, she told the Urban Rehabilitation Standards Board: "We know that our neighborhood doesn't mean much to you, but it's all we have."

This Tuesday night, at the community meeting, Charlie Jackson has much to talk about: there are problems with homes red-tagged by city code officials, which means they are one step shy of being demolished. Jackson says some of them truly do need to be reduced to rubble, but some of them truly do need to be brought back from the dead. There are problems with insurance people preying on the old people in Joppa. There are still problems with "contractors" who say they can update the wooden houses and who would probably foreclose on the elderly owners if they couldn't keep up their payments. There is still a problem getting past the trains that seal off the neighborhood's main exit.

In the pews of Gethsemane Baptist, Audray Jackson listens and nods her head. Just a few weeks ago, an ambulance came for the twenty-five-year-old's uncle after he had a stroke. She rode with him until the ambulance skidded to a halt, waiting for a train to move. She jumped outside and screamed at the conductor. For what seemed like forever, the ambulance honked its horn and blew its siren, but the train wouldn't budge. Finally, her uncle made it to the hospital; people in Joppa say there have been others over the years who weren't so lucky. Audray's uncle is still in Baylor Medical Center.

There is also still a problem with vacant homes being torched, just as there was back in the 1970s, when some residents believed there was a conspiracy to drive black people away from Joppa, to secure this hidden land and make something of it. There is a problem with getting city crews to clean up the streets. A problem with getting sidewalks installed. Problems with faulty electrical service.

"I don't think we have got our share," argues longtime Joppa resident Lizzie Crowder, seventy-five. "We need sidewalks, we need new streets. We haven't gotten our share of the things the city does for other people. You can see for yourself. Do you think we are getting our share?"

James King, the seventy-five-year-old man sitting straight and staring alertly ahead in one of those Gethsemane Baptist pews, doesn't think he has gotten his share. He has lived on Yukon Street since the end of World War II, and he still has no running water. Still has no sewage service. He still tends to an old well that sits in the middle of his front yard. All because a water main stops 200 feet from his house, and the City of Dallas says he must pay to have the line extended.

From King's front yard, he can see through the faded trees toward another problem that he, Charlie Jackson, and some of the others say haunts Joppa. The Sleepy Hollow Country Club, which sits to the east and south of Joppa, has been its neighbor for four decades. Today, the club is tied to a thread of property that snakes away from the golf course and into the heart of Joppa. Part of that wooded, impassable property, in effect, slices some of Joppa's streets in half. For years, the residents have been trying to strike a deal with the club: give up that land so that a bridge can be built. So that bus service can go into the community. So that the elderly don't have to walk a mile to see their children. Larry Duncan, who served as a city councilman, told me: "It's no secret that the country club wants to run them out. [Joppa residents] are in a war with a white, moneyed, country-club golf course."

The head of Sleepy Hollow sees it differently. Charles Tabor tells me, "I don't know of any other business that is attracting 400 white people to this area."

After years spent studying research on the area's geography and demographics, he thinks all of Joppa should be condemned. "If there is anything worse than that in Dallas, I've not seen it. We really wish it would just go away. I'm not the white male racist son of a bitch. I'm really not. I just have a little perspective," the country club owner says.

Later he adds: "They ought to bulldoze that place in the middle of the night."

Joppa's problems aren't new ones. "The entire south half of this city has been neglected historically. And Joppa is a special place because they have been there longer," Duncan tells me. "They have been there since shortly after the Civil War. Most people in this city do not know about that proud history. But you can see that it is a deep-rooted community. They are very much self-reliant. They are used to doing things for themselves. That history has left its mark. They don't aspire to be North Dallas. They just want to be what they are."

Laurabelle Foster carried the fight as long as she could. So did the Reverend I. L. Callicut, who worked for years as an elevator operator at the downtown Neiman Marcus while also serving as acting president of the South Central Civic League. And now Charlie Jackson has taken the lead. Today, it is her dining-room table that all the maps are splayed out on. The papers are piled high. The petitions are signed. Here is the plan to raise the money to open the old pool in South Central Park after the City of Dallas said it couldn't spend the $700. Here is where people signed up to tear down the old Jefferson house—before the city charged the family to do it for them. Here is where Charlie concocted a plan for people to flood city hall with phone calls one morning to demand cleanups and the construction of a bridge, which she wants named Laurabelle Foster Crossing.

Here, Charlie Mae Jackson tries to figure out where the money will come from for a local children's football team and how the community can fix up old Pierce Field. Here is where she meets with the community-liaison police officers the city has assigned to Joppa.

And this is where Charlie Jackson worries whether the grinding force of

Dallas development will finally reach out and smite Joppa down—erase it and make it available for someone other than the children of freed slaves.

"We live in a cruel society, where friends are no longer friends. Where neighbors are no longer neighbors, and human life is not worth ten cents. Where in the world have we gotten?" I hear her plead with the forty people of Joppa on that Tuesday night inside the church. "I know it's hot out there . . . I know it's real hot. But . . . give me an hour . . . two hours . . . just give me a helping hand," she says. "Joppa is not just a place between the railroad tracks and the highway."

For a few painfully long seconds, there is an awful silence in the church. The only sound is the lonesome whirring of the ceiling fans slowly cutting the air.

"Do you feel like we are doing the right thing?" implores Charlie, looking from face to face, her fingers wrapped around her papers.

Finally, a tender mercy.

There is the sound of one person clapping.

Another.

And then several more.

Edgar Green, who has lived forty-two of his forty-four years in Joppa, unfolds his arms and raises one hand: "Let's take the levee down out there and flood that golf course. We need a good place to fish, boat, and resort!" he yells.

Standing at the front of the church next to Charlie, her young aide-de-camp, Denise Fowler, is smiling. She once served on the Wilmer-Hutchins school board, and now she spends much of her time visiting the sages of Joppa: The Reverend A. W. Blair, the quietly elegant man who kept one eye on the Klan meeting hall across the highway and who built the second church in Joppa, in the early 1940s. Gracie Burrell, ninety-four, the oldest resident in Joppa and someone who traces a direct line back to the first freed slaves who carved out an existence along Honey Springs. The Reverend Callicut, who at eighty-nine says he is the oldest precinct judge in Dallas and who now rails against the men in ties and with clipboards who claim they can give him loans to fix his house.

"Get off my property!" Callicut's neighbors hear him roaring.

These are the people of Joppa.

The people who, like the freedmen they are descended from, know that in America, true wealth is the land, even a hidden land, a place haunted by echoes.

And now, in the old Gethsemane Baptist Church, where many of these people worship, Charlie Jackson is beaming. Her body seems to surge to life at the sense of community on this hot August night.

"Thank you," she says, her voice booming against the ancient walls of the church, booming louder than those echoes from the woods. "For a minute, I thought I was in this alone."

For years, Joppa existed in some sort of forgotten, neglected limbo. Attention turned Joppa's way in the twenty-first century, and city officials and historians who have studied the neighborhood say Joppa might actually be saved. It is mentioned in various controversial plans the city has been exploring for improving broad areas around the Trinity River—and some residents were relieved that, at least, Joppa wasn't automatically designated for demolition.

SAND
BRANCH
BLUES

Most mornings, I would meet the photographer David Leeson at a little convenience store, as they call them in Texas, in south Dallas County. I would buy something for breakfast, and we would climb inside his jeep and ride down the road to Sand Branch, passing by the yawning wastewater treatment plant. We would ride the blocks, and then we would walk them. There seemed to be a sense of gratitude, in a way, that we were there. Maybe his jeep suggested that some action was going to finally take place. Maybe it was his official-looking camera gear. Me with the notebook. David, if I remember, was also using a small Leica he had put on his belt. Something unobtrusive. He knew about gaining trust. Far more, as it turned out, than I did. Years later, he would finally win a Pulitzer for his work.

Sand Branch was almost too evident. People would approach us with shopping carts filled with empty water bottles. The poisoned water, literally, was in the well. There was raw sewage. We never really talked, as far as I know, about when the story would end, when we should stop working on it. We knew we could have stayed there forever; we knew we could have stopped reporting and come back in a year, and it would still be exactly the same. Jesse Jackson had called the Sugar Ditch area of Tunica, Mississippi, "America's Ethiopia." We weren't sure what to call Sand Branch. The story, when it appeared, generated an enormous response—donations, volunteer efforts, clothing drives. And David quietly returned, with carpenters and other workers, to repair homes. I had noticed, while we were visiting people in Sand Branch, that he made a point of asking for the birth dates of the children. I thought he wanted to be extra accurate when he mentioned their ages in his photo cutlines. He was asking so he could get the children birthday presents. In Sand Branch, it seemed as if people had reached some nadir, and they had that same weary gaze you see in refugee camps around the world. We could see the Dallas skyline every time we turned our backs on Sand Branch.

From inside, in the smothering heat and darkness of the falling-down shack, the battered screen door could be heaven's gate. A storm is rolling in from the west, and gray, grave light is shooting through the ripped mesh. Irma Webb, sweating and sweet faced, stands in a corner of her flimsy house. She stares at the bundle of eerie rays and waits for rain. She wants to talk about her mother's death, about how Mama didn't have to suffer, at least not like the people she left behind in Sand Branch, one of America's most forgotten corners.

Irma had hoped her mother would live as long as Grandma Clara, who celebrated 100 birthdays. People used to say Grandma was living on somebody else's time, but Irma always insisted that Grandma was definitely living on her own time. Mama passed away years ago at the age of seventy-one, and Irma still sees it unfolding.

Irma is sitting by her mother's bedside at Methodist Hospital down in Dallas. "You pray for me, you hear?" Mama whispers to her daughter.

"I will," replies Irma.

At two in the morning, Mama turns her back, maybe to keep her children from seeing the last breath leave her body.

Irma thinks that watching someone die is almost like seeing all the air pressed out of a paper bag. When she finally looks, her mother's face is frozen in a smile.

As Irma talks about Mama, a weak, naked lightbulb from another room barely illuminates one side of her body. A mound of rotting garbage outside, one of many festering piles dotting this part of Texas, is burning, and the acrid smoke is moving over everything, snaking through the door screen. The smell deadens, flattens the air. Three blocks away, a neighbor is begging for potable water: he is walking down a baking street, through that haze, asking people whether they have water to spare. A family of twelve shoehorned into a shotgun shack is using a plastic gallon bucket for a toilet. Someone in that family tells people they poured gasoline on the animals they thought had cholera and set them on fire. It is near dusk in Sand Branch, an amiably named zone a few feet from the southeastern city limits of Dallas, America's seventh-largest city. It could be a Depression-era shantytown or a squalid mountain village in Honduras.

Irma grew up in the country, washed her clothes by hand, grew her own food. She has raised so many children in Sand Branch, including several who were just left with her, that she has lost count. Maybe twenty, maybe twenty-five. Some children came to stay with her when a foster daughter ran off. "About two years ago I got four more," she says.

Today the sixty-four-year-old has a baby tucked under her arm and a thin layer of moisture on her forehead. She has a soft voice and a quiet strength. "I want to die like my mother," she tells me. "I don't want to suffer."

Irma's low, waterlogged ceiling is splintered and sagging. Electrical wires dangle out of rotting holes and touch my head. Tacked to the cracked walls are an old photograph of Dr. Martin Luther King, Jr., a photo of the JFK motorcade in Dallas on the day the president died, and a faded portrait of Kennedy with the barely visible message: "Ask not what your country can do for you . . ."

Rainwater skids from the ceiling to the buckled plank floor. Whenever water comes from the skies, older people smile. For decades, the thirsty have coaxed their water out of the earth. Some still lure it with creaky hand pumps; the people without pumps rely on friends. But by the 1980s, dozens of the wells had become dangerously poisoned, and their owners began to haul water from miles away—as if a shimmering, humming metropolis with a fountain of water in front of the new Dallas City Hall was not just down the road. As if this was somewhere out of sight and beyond time. As if Sand Branch didn't really exist.

There are plastic buckets and jugs everywhere—just like the ones I saw on Smoky Mountain, the giant, rolling landfill in Manila where people had set up homes and used buckets for everything imaginable. Like the ones I saw in Esteli, in northern Nicaragua, where people scavenged the buckets for rain, for fuel, for everything imaginable. Clorox jugs, plastic vats that once held laundry soap or dog food, plastic soda bottles with faded labels, some without tops—and all of them used to gather up drinking water, to house bathing water, to use for wastewater. Hundreds of plastic buckets, tossed here and there, tucked alongside homes, underneath leaning bungalows, as if this was an old, battered coastal town and cheap, crumbling buoys or life preservers were accumulating everywhere.

In Sand Branch, the simple act of raising a cup of water, maybe badly contaminated water, to your lips is never far from your mind. There is no sewer service. Unfathomably—because this is what some see as the prosperous tail end of the twentieth century—typhoid, cholera, dysentery, and maybe even plague threaten the residents. There are outhouses. People let raw sewage fall underneath their homes. There is no refuse pickup. No fire hydrants, buses, parks, streetlights, sidewalks, or curbs. Dallas's massive Southside Wastewater Treatment Plant is across the street, processing all the sludge in Dallas, 120 tons sent daily from every corner of the exponentially growing city.

In Sand Branch, needs are elemental. And there is an intimately detailed, specific need that transcends all else. It is the thing that makes this place resemble those places that emerge for a minute or two, now and then, on the evening news. Those dusty hellholes, usually in Africa . . . somewhere else . . . where the children have want etched in their faces and their lips are cracked. Where people's lives have been reduced to something pointed, something simple but completely unattainable: something to eat . . . some water to drink.

In Sand Branch, all the blights dim alongside the day-to-day need to fill a drinking glass with water. Try to go there in the dead of summer, realizing that the heat is rising up out of the sand and into the soles of your shoes, and know there is no water to drink. And so, when a sudden shower interrupts the dry summer, it is cruelly providential. As sure as that rain will bloat nearby Hickory Creek and Parson's Slough, water will also snake its way through Sand Branch's humble roofs. Sometimes it will thunder down so hard that people wonder whether the 100-year flood has finally come to splinter the Bois D'Arc Levee, the line of copper-colored earth that holds back the sorrowful, capricious Trinity River. Maybe, people say, this time the levee won't hold. Maybe this time God will send his cleansing anger and wash Sand Branch away. Everyone else has an ulterior motive when it comes to Sand Branch. It is the poorest, most isolated place in Dallas County— maybe in the country—and it has been a pawn in a quiet high-stakes political game involving millions of dollars and powerful interest groups. Everyone else has an ulterior motive regarding the people in Sand Branch—why not God?

"I believe that if you ask for something from your heart, you'll get your wish," says Irma, still rocking the tiny baby in her arms. Together we stand in the dark, still waiting for rain. I see her face in profile, like a faded sepia-toned photograph in a cameo locket.

She wants to die like her mother, but first she wants something else.

"I'm asking that God will send us a little help and strength so that we can get out of this place. So that we can get a better place before we leave this world."

The Bottom is the place for people who hold the Brahmin's hem. In Texas—from the Fifth Ward in Houston to small towns along the Navasota River, from far East San Antonio to tiny places like Elmo or Frogtown—people talk about living in The Bottom or The Bottoms. It is an area, an outpost, a bunker, a place of exile—and a state of mind. It is mentioned in conversation, in song. It can be "on the other side of the tracks," but it often refers to the lowlands down by riverbanks and creek beds. The areas where the poor—for an aching, thorny nest of complex reasons—have been sent through all of American history. It is there in Tyler and Killeen and Marshall; it is there all along the gumbo-soil areas near Buffalo Bayou and West Dallas Street in Houston; it is there right in the shadow of Houston's hanging tree, outside the city cemetery where the city founders were buried . . . and you could even slip beyond Texas . . . say you found yourself in Sugar Ditch, Mississippi, you could tell yourself it would all be like some figures that you suddenly see reappearing outside your car window, some frayed person, almost shapeless and without angles and as if they, it, were waiting for that final air to ease out of them. As if a strong wind could blow and everyone and everything, all that ill-constructed flimsiness, would just crumble away.

First to flood, first to be touched by tuberculosis, first to be forgotten, The Bottom is not just stuck in time, it is somewhere beyond time, as if the past were eternal, as if the future held no prospect of change. Stripped of any cushion of reference points, you will be hard pressed to name the year. In Texas, in America, now, it is as if you are looking through a smoky prism, the edges washed out and the details so unfocused and, yes, so bittersweet that it has to be an invention. There is a thick, unyielding quality to The Bottom, like some ponderous Renaissance-era oil painting . . . this world that exists only inside its borders, with muted light, with shadows, with whispers, stripped of any hint of newness or hope for reinvention. It is, in the end, timeless.

Sand Branch is in The Bottom. It is The Bottom, one of those spiritually, culturally, historically connected places in Texas. Sand Branch is at the heart of a 100-year floodplain, only yards from the Trinity River. Before and after World War II, a calculating developer took some small frame houses in Dallas and deposited them on undesirable, cheap, and sandy land then twenty miles from the city limits. Blacks, along with a handful of white and Hispanic families, quickly moved to the inexpensive opportunities offered by Sand Branch—and away from the obvious limitations of the inner city. African Americans in rural Texas were seeing their sons go off to war, so families needed work, maybe work near big cities like Dallas. After the war, returning servicemen wanted their own homes, and they wanted to work near cities. People relocating to the Dallas area from the still-rising sorrows of East Texas and northern Louisiana headed to Sand Branch, even with the constant threat of an apocalyptic flood.

It was a place to own affordable land. To take title to your first house in a secluded, rural world. Where you could dig holes for cedar posts and tap into cool water that could be sipped as it gurgled from the ground.

Water, *everywhere*.

Through the 1940s and 1950s, word of mouth spread, the way things can sometimes do surprisingly quickly in a state as big as Texas. Two branches of the King family moved there. The Offords. The Livingstons. The Smiths. The Whitlows. Old Man Turner ran the grocery store. And Old Man Turner was like the gatekeeper, the man in the lighthouse, because he dug all the water wells with his son. He was on time, people said. He was on time. He knew there was water under Sand Branch, and he knew how to summon it.

Henrietta King, born in Shreveport, went to Sand Branch after she had first moved to South Dallas in 1948. The Jewish families that defined South Dallas, like the Marcus family, the family that lent its name to the famous Neiman Marcus store, were already beginning to leave for the north side of the river. But after only two years of city life, she decided she needed to be in the country. She heard about Sand Branch and, yes, about the water. She found a simple wooden house, and she found work "pulling greens" for two dollars a day at O. B. Howard's truck farm. Big, fine, fat mounds of mustard and collard greens that were destined for farmers' markets around Texas, for the vendors who still patrolled the streets with vegetable and fruit wagons.

She washed with a rubboard, knuckles skidding over the metal, and she cooked on a wood stove and picked wild berries from areas around Parson's Slough. She grew watermelons, learning to beat the vines with sticks in case snakes had curled up inside the tangles and pregnant clumps of weeds. There was a rhythm. She gathered pecans, and she raised just enough chickens for meat and eggs. She had goats. And through it all, her son, Junior Nonesuch, burned his feet on the hot sand, as fine as sugar, running barefoot in the summer. It wasn't Eden, it wasn't the land of milk and honey, but it was a little bit like an oasis. There was sand everywhere, and there was water under that sand. And Junior Nonesuch would run, and then he would raise a jug of well water, as cool as if it had been kept on the back porch in early December, to his lips. He would squat by the side of the unpaved road and watch city kids drag-racing their cars over the flatlands.

Junior knew that if his mother ever needed to deal with the powers that be, things in Sand Branch worked like a southern plantation. She would go to Mr. Charlie, the nickname people used for the handful of white farmers who lorded over the area, and Mr. Charlie would take care of it. Years ago, Junior also began to think of Sand Branch as Tobacco Road, a village of people who knew that their homes, their community, were always marooned outside the gilded tent. "You know that song? 'Tobacco Road, it's just a home, it's just a home,'" Junior says to me one afternoon while peering out at Sand Branch through a fog of cigarette smoke.

Around the corner, Sallie Smith had bought a little plot of land with her husband. Born the day after New Year's in 1910, she grew up in a family of twenty-two in West Texas, near Lorenzo. She and her husband, Bennie, moved to Sand Branch to be closer to his mother. He went to work at the cotton gin in Ferris. She kept a few hogs and sold eggs, okra, onions, tomatoes, cucumbers, and corn; she washed the sand off the goods, wrapped the produce in blankets, and sold it door to door, fanning out the items as if she were offering up gleaming gems. She never went up and never went down on the price of her eggs: they were fifty cents a dozen. The money was important, and Sallie was proud she never had to borrow from Mr. Charlie or anybody else. But she always knew how close to the edge everyone lived. She always knew how fate, circumstance, and some dark poetry could lead somewhere bad.

"I don't want no comeback talk, that's why I pay as I go. It is hard in Sand Branch. If you don't have no way to make it, you are just plain o-u-t," she says.

The churches came almost as quickly as the residents. The Wayside Church. Mount Zion Church. And other things, too, fell in line. The kinds of things that anchor a place in time. Miss Bell opened up a small candy store. Miss Burton served up barbecue at a little stand. A semblance of a community took shape.

And, of course, there was always one constant. One thing that people could truly depend on. The water in Sand Branch was good enough to cook with. To bathe in. To swim in. To drink. To baptize your babies with.

People in the city heard the news about Sand Branch. Lemon Webb, Irma's husband, had lived just below the levee in West Dallas. That was another place everyone called The Bottom. That was where the Trinity River turned mean, worse than capricious: swollen with brackish water, carrying dead animals all the way from the farms near Fort Worth, and pockmarked by eddies that simply sucked a man down. The great blues-man T-Bone Walker made the Trinity River the subject of a recording. It was all about surviving the river, getting away from the river, being exiled to live alongside the river. It was called "Trinity River Blues": "That dirty Trinity River sure have done me wrong, / It came in my windows and doors . . . / . . . believe I'm going to lose my mind."

And Lemon Webb just wanted out of West Dallas. It was hell there. West Dallas was like some foreign zone on American soil. Earnest sociologists and "urban affairs experts" from Chicago and New York would take "field trips" to West Dallas. They had heard there was this pocket close to downtown that was filled with disease, abject poverty, people working in choking cement plants and in conditions worse than any of the things Upton Sinclair had seen and written about. Everyone in West Dallas, it seemed, knew someone who was sick or dying. It was like some dark Eastern European industrial town after World War II, with smoke, soot, and shacks fanning out from the brooding factories. Lemon wanted out. He planned a move to Sand Branch.

And he wasn't alone. Donald Scott was in South Dallas, watching that neighborhood become neglected and forgotten, and he saw Chicago Red, who was said to be a thief and a gangster, getting organized, and Red was beginning to get things going even more than he had back in the 1950s. Scott wanted out. He was tired of sidestepping the gangsters—and the Dallas cops, including the one they called Mad Dog. Scott was tired of it all, tired of the gangsters coming through his house "like Grand Central Station." He wanted to retreat to the country, and he followed the trail south to Sand Branch.

Never incorporated, never big enough to have its own census tract, Sand Branch grew until 400 to 500 people lived there. Life along the unpaved roads expanded quietly, isolated from any county services. People were self-sufficient in part because they had to be, in part because they wanted to be. Others heard about the cheap land in Sand Branch: hog farmers, many of whom lived elsewhere in Dallas County, bought plots in the middle of the residential sections. Next to people's homes they erected flimsy, sprawling pens—like ones I had seen in desolate regions of El Salvador or Honduras—made out of scrap metal and cardboard.

Every few days the hog farmers arrived with trucks loaded down with slop: rotting apples, orange peels, okra, greens. They would back the trucks to the pens, unload, and leave. Low-lying pockets filled up with mosquitoes, stagnant water, feces, urine. When the animals showed signs of illnesses, people said it was cholera and that the hogs had to be set on fire.

And then there were other people and things coming to Sand Branch. In time, and no one is exactly sure when it started, strangers began appearing with clipboards, surveying equipment, and metal rods that they speared into the sand. They squatted down alongside their pickup trucks, scooped up dollops of earth, and put it in jars. They held the jars up to the light and made marks on them. Parents in Sand Branch found themselves yanking their children back from the paths of a bulldozer—and then more trucks, and then some earth haulers. The trucks and the men in mirrored sunglasses fanned out across the empty patches of land around Sand Branch until it seemed that they had encircled the community. No one was sure the day it started, but by the 1960s and on into the 1970s, the trucks became omnipresent. Aggregate—the sand and pebbles that are mixed with cement to make concrete—was being discovered everywhere in and around Sand Branch.

The very thing that Sand Branch was built on, the substance that gave the town its name, became an enormously valuable commodity as Dallas began its explosive lurch forward—and as the Dallas city limits began creeping toward Sand Branch.

At first it was a slowly escalating process. But through the 1970s, gravel pits began to scar the area's face. Their spread kept pace with Dallas's and Texas's boom until the quarries squeezing Sand Branch were supplying 90 percent of the aggregate mined in Dallas County. As Dallas and Houston grew larger and larger, as each new skyscraper was built, as fresh, gleaming suburbs were built, as megachurches were developed . . . and shopping malls and new roads and new sidewalks and new libraries were built . . . much of the material flowed from Sand Branch's bedrock. The city and much of the state, without question, were built with the very essence of Sand Branch. The pebbles and rocks that held Sand Branch together were being scooped up, and all the noise and hum and clatter of those rocks piling into metallic trucks beds were like some cacophonous prelude to a welling nightmare.

When each quarry was tapped out, when the huge scoopers could not lift out any more aggregate, or when pockets of underground water were hit, the gravel men quickly moved to another spot. There were gouges, craters, all around the fragile homes in Sand Branch. A few at first, then dozens, maybe hundreds of craters. And when the rains came, the rainwater filled the craters to overflowing, and even more plagues of mosquitoes covered the scummed ponds.

In the late 1970s, the first hints arrived: people bending over their backyard water pumps, stooping down to sip the cool water that they had summoned out of the ground for fifty years, knew that something was not quite right. There was something wrong with the one thing they could always have faith in. The water—Sand Branch's reason for being—was going bad as the pastureland around the community disappeared. The spiritually inclined, the men and women who saw a divine hand at work—a higher power, a presence, that had delivered people from bad things in the city and straight to quiet, self-sufficient, and, yes, blessed, Sand Branch—began to wonder whether the Creator was testing them. *Why give something to the people . . . and then poison it, take it back? It had to be a divine test.*

Ira Ruff, an energetic woman who worked at a health clinic, saw it and tasted it. "We always had a little sand in the water, but this was bad." From the front windows of her small, neat home, Ms. Ruff watched the rocks spitting out from the tires of the gravel trucks roaring down the narrow stretch of Beltline Road. She began dwelling on the idea that things happened to Sand Branch as if no one really lived there.

It was something she thought about even more when Dallas began expanding the Southside Wastewater Treatment Plant, a huge operation that separated Sand Branch from its view of the Dallas skyline. Each time she saw additional work going on at the plant, she knew her fate—and the fate of all of Sand Branch—was sealed: who would ever want to buy property in the odious shadow of one of the largest wastewater plants in the country?

And she was also worried about something more immediate. Like her neighbors, she was concerned that the massive plant would eat away at the purity of Sand Branch's water. Through the early 1980s, the smell from the tons of sludge was sickening enough—wasn't there a chance that the sludge would seep down and harm the underground water supply?

One thing she was sure of: Dallas and Texas were growing on the back of Sand Branch. Downtown buildings, expensive homes—maybe even the 2,000-acre wastewater plant servicing the sleek, new northern areas of Dallas—were using Sand Branch's bedrock. Sand Branch, some said, was being used so Dallas could grow. And it looked, to people like Ira Ruff, as though Sand Branch was offering up its lifeblood.

"They are killing us," she told me one day.

The orange trees were always something. Going to Los Angeles every year to visit relatives who had fled Texas for California—following the huge migration that many black Texans had made, in direct contrast to the black residents of Mississippi and other southern states who had migrated north to

Detroit and Chicago—Lemon Webb could never get over the fact that there would just be fruit on the ground.

Lemon hasn't been to LA in several years. He has heart and lung trouble, and it makes him laugh the way the young doctors and nurses at Parkland Hospital, where President Kennedy's body had been taken, scold him about taking better care of himself. Lemon's voice has shriveled to a whisper. If he needs to raise it—as when Ashley or one of his other grandchildren meanders too close to the speeding gravel trucks—he arches his thin body and reaches deep within himself. When he yells, he almost seems to surprise himself. Like a lot of people in Sand Branch, he makes the forty-five-minute trip to Parkland because he can't afford to go anywhere closer. He plans his visits this way: "Pack a lunch because you don't know how long you'll have to wait."

The people who rent the leaky-roofed house next door for $100 a month stood silently at the fence and watched him one day. Lemon couldn't breathe, and an ambulance had somehow arrived and was loading him to Parkland. Now that he is back home, he spends his days on a small cot. He shares his cramped area with one of the teenagers Irma is raising. The boy sleeps on an old, damp couch. Six children live in an adjacent room. Irma, her daughters, and other grandchildren stay in a side room. They worry about the collapsing ceiling, praying that it doesn't crush one of the babies in the middle of the night. When it rains, Lemon puts a bucket on his bed to catch the water.

In the early 1990s, the Webbs finally paid off the $3,000 their house and land cost them when they moved to Sand Branch in 1961. Irma's family had roots in the South Texas countryside, and Lemon's family had come from northern Louisiana. He always liked the outdoors, always thought it was good for people, for kids. "It runs in my blood," the retired plumber whispers to me. "All the people on my father's side were farmers."

Now he pools his Social Security checks with Irma's, and they get about $700 a month. They receive foods stamps and another $300 from the Aid to Families with Dependent Children program. Other family members pitch in what they can; the total pays for propane, electricity, food, and clothing for themselves, their children, and their natural and foster grandchildren. The $1,200 or so each month goes to support, in the end, as many as fifteen people.

Almost 80 percent of the people in Sand Branch survive on Social Security or welfare; almost 30 percent are at or below the poverty level. Many troop into the tiny Sand Branch grocery store and simply lay money on the counter—they can't count or read. Almost a third of the adults in Sand

Branch are unemployed. Half of Sand Branch's housing is either dilapidated or deteriorated. A study completed by county inspectors in 1987 dryly talks about homes like the Webbs' this way: "These structures also represent constant, tangible proof of a hemorrhaging community. As such, the psychological damage that these reminders might inflict may just be as debilitating as any physical injury."

Watching the brownish water come through their roof one Tuesday afternoon, Lemon and Irma have little time for psychological assessments, melancholy, or false hopes. They have to deal with water—water they want, water they don't want, the maddening, sickening circle of water. Fetid water, no water, wastewater, polluted water, potable water, water falling on the bed, water not coming out of the pumps, larvae wriggling in the water, finding plastic jugs for water, who last had water for a bath, whether the water should be boiled, whether the water should be bottled, who has water they can borrow, what can they barter for some water.

Irma's mother had gone to her grave raising children. And Irma still remembers how the family brought her father back from Parkland Hospital and buried him in the family plot in the South Texas town of Yoakum. Now, with no water, she has other things on her mind. Nothing makes sense—at least nothing people, including me, tell her.

"The only thing you really know are the things you can see before your eyes," she tells me one day. "I go by my eyes and ears. That's the only way you know exactly what is happening."

In the 1990s, Sand Branch saw a swirl of strangers. Even the news people have come again, as they have every so often in the past. "It's like the natives and the missionaries," says Andy Riley, who tries to get his $100 a month rent knocked down whenever rain bursts through his shack at the edge of a rusted scrap heap on Beltline Road.

"You all are the missionaries, and we are the natives. I tell you what—I'm just as curious about you as you are of me. You all are from a different world than Sand Branch. You just cross the city line," he says, pointing down the road, "and it's a whole different way of life here."

Some missionaries seem to realize that fact.

"It is a Third World–country community. It has to be one of the worst you have ever seen. As bad as the projects are in Dallas, Chicago, New York, Los Angeles, at least they have running water," Rick Loessberg, a Dallas County coordinator for planning and development, tells me.

"I can't believe this type of situation exists. It's not a comfortable feeling when you go through the community," adds Chester Vaughn, the Dallas County environmental health director.

"I thought I was in another world just fifteen minutes from downtown Dallas," says Glen McGee, a county environmental health officer who monitors Sand Branch.

"The only thing that I have seen that is worse is Sugar Ditch, Mississippi," says County Commissioner John Wiley Price, referring to the area that a few years ago symbolized the most wretched face of rural poverty in America—a place that Reverend Jesse Jackson had called "America's Ethiopia."

Dallas puffed itself out through the 1970s and 1980s until it bumped into smaller bits of Texas like Lancaster, DeSoto, Mesquite, Addison, and several more. Through the 1990s and beyond, Dallas and Texas began dispatching their surveyors and analysts to fine-comb Sand Branch. The unincorporated area can simply be snapped up, without a vote, whenever Dallas is ready to take it. For years there has been talk that Dallas needs a third airport—or maybe one to replace venerable Love Field. Maybe it could go in Sand Branch.

In the corridors of the I. M. Pei–designed city hall—an angular, thrusting building that seems as clinical and frigid as a gleaming scalpel resting alone on a surgical tray—Sand Branch has been debated ad nauseam. The discussions have centered not on how to fix it, but on what it stands in the way of: airports and even billion-dollar projects to resculpt the Trinity River.

Irma Webb, who has lived for so long on the other side of the giant wastewater moat that separates Sand Branch from a major American city, isn't sure what it all means. She wonders whether Dallas will just take over Sand Branch some day. Maybe that would be good, but to many, the thought runs counter to why people escaped to Sand Branch in the first place.

"If it means a better world . . . ," she says, her soft voice trailing off.

"If the city takes Sand Branch over, how the hell are people going to afford to bring their house up to all the different city codes? People out here cannot even afford water and food," yells Joe Robinson, who runs the humble Sand Branch Grocery on Beltline Road.

And meanwhile, at the end of a brutal unpaved road, Donald Scott is leaning forward in a chair inside his trailer home. He is holding a drinking glass coated with a slick, filmy scum. "My water went bad when the wastewater plant started expanding," he says.

As he holds his glass, he wonders whether Dallas is really just after the sand gravel under the homes of Sand Branch—the remaining bits of aggregate that haven't yet been mined. He wonders whether the city is just out to expand the wastewater plant. Or whether it really is all about a new airport that has to be built to accommodate all those people who have moved to Dallas, who are moving to Dallas. It is like a superheated circle, flames all around . . . Sand Branch helps Dallas grow, Dallas's growth sucks Sand Branch dry, and, finally, Dallas grows so large that it has to consume the water, the earth, and everything in and around Sand Branch—and the place simply vanishes. Scott doesn't believe Dallas wants to annex Sand Branch just so it will become legally required to spend millions of dollars for a water supply, fire hydrants, garbage pickup, a sewer system, buses, and streetlights—let alone the estimated $8 million it would cost to truly protect Sand Branch from a 100-year flood. There has to be something else, some other reason for the interest in Sand Branch.

"Why bother doing all that stuff? What do they want to do with us?" Scott asks me as he holds his contaminated glass up to the light.

A few blocks away, Airlene Bradford takes a break at a shack on Lake Street that passes for a community center. In this small building, Bradford and others hand out "commodities" to the needy. No one from the city, county, or state has ever mentioned anything to her about a possible airport. She heard about it from a friend one day when she was out hauling trash. She thinks she has the answer to Donald Scott's questions.

"If they want to run us out, they can figure out how to do it," she tells me.

Crews at the wastewater treatment plant are busy draining gravel pits adjacent to Sand Branch. They are pits purchased from legendary Texas millionaire Clint Murchison—famous for owning the Dallas Cowboys, being the heir to an oil fortune, spending millions on schemes to convert manure into something useful, womanizing, and fraternizing with the biggest power brokers and shadiest backdoor characters in Texas. It would make sense that Murchison, one of the unyielding and over-the-top empire builders in the state, would reach far below the cloud line and leave his fingerprints on Sand Branch. In Texas, if you labor at it, you can discover the lines that connect one end of the caste system to another. Each end is, in the end, defined by its relationship—its history—with the others.

One fact became indisputable in the 1990s: county studies showed that dozens of Sand Branch wells had been badly tainted by coliform organisms. Maggie Livingston's water. Sherry Crockett's. Callie Wedlow's. Oweda Johnson's. Robert Cook's. Emmett Thomas's. Margaret Adams's. Edward Rivers's. Ninety percent of the wells were contaminated.

Even the politicians sensed something larger and immutable at work. Some unforgiving, bruising collaboration of forces, history, people, and politics. "That treatment plant is out there by design. It is not an irony. When they were building the plant, they knew Sand Branch existed. So what? It is just another poor community," county commissioner Price told me one day. "Even if Sand Branch was Anglo, they still wouldn't give a damn. It is just a poor community filled with people just trying to exist. They can't turn a spigot on and get water. Where can they get the strength to fight a giant wastewater treatment plant?"

And in the end, erasing the entire community of Sand Branch—erasing a place that African Americans had come to call their own, that residents had seen as self-directed, a place that began with a taproot emerging from cool, clear water—may cost less money than trying to cure it.

O n a miserable rainy afternoon, the Webbs are also worried about money and curing things, fixing things. Right now, a dozen family members are under the shredded, leaking roof. The water pump has been broken for three weeks, and even if it were working, no one knew exactly what would come streaming forth. They can't afford the $160 to fix the pump. They hope a nephew will bring out some water for the toilet. Overnight, another hole opened up in the ceiling. Lemon filled up two ten-gallon buckets with rain coming toward his narrow bed. The water has gnarled the floor planks and left the room moldy and damp.

Slumped on a couch set against the blackened walls of his room, Lemon seems smaller and more worried than before. The eighty-year-old repeatedly presses a bony hand to his forehead. He has a fever. Irma lowers herself, with a sigh, into a cracked chair and watches him. She looks deeply, intensely tired. She tossed and turned all night worrying about the ceiling—whether it would come down on the babies and how she could find the money to fix it.

For a minute, it is almost quiet. The children are huddled on the floor of the dank kitchen, fighting with the fire ants for their macaroni and cheese. Since the neighbors got a batch of cats, there have been fewer rats in the house.

I'm not sure I've been in the presence of someone who seems more guaranteed to move beyond that battered screen door, to pass through that heaven's gate.

"It's good to hang on to things sometimes. But sometimes it's good to let them go," says Irma as she keeps an eye on her sweating husband. "I think I'm ready to let go of all this."

After I first wrote about Sand Branch in the 1990s, there was an ironic deluge— a veritable flood of cash, checks, and goodwill. Volunteers from around the state came to help repair homes, to see whether they could dig new water wells, to see whether they could give food, clothing, anything, to the people in Sand Branch. For years, good-hearted people kept coming. They tried to change things, home by home. But in the end, no deep, systemic solutions for Sand Branch were ever found. Residents still struggled to get water. The housing stock and population dwindled, but no significant civic improvements were made. The planned airport was never built. The area was never annexed by Dallas; some people said that Dallas simply didn't want to bear the expense of healing it. Sand Branch remains one of the most neglected places outside a major urban area in America.

FIRE IN THE HOLE BLUES

I liked to take the long way home, sometimes south down Oakland (now Malcolm X) and then a right on Martin Luther King, Jr. Boulevard, aiming for Oak Cliff, crossing a dank leg of the Trinity River and then cutting back by the Dallas Zoo. One night I stopped on the dark bridge over the river. There was some strange creature at the side of the road. I thought it was a nutria or some biochemical creation from the depths of the polluted water. It was a dog, coated with mange, bleeding from sores. I drove away, cursed, did a U-turn, and picked up the dog. I went to an all-night vet's office and had the dog more or less revived. It was a little like another random day on MLK when I was driving toward Oakland. Near where Jasper Baccus had once chased me into the street, thinking I was a fraud, an imposter. There was something on fire in the alley. Something back there. I did a U-turn. I stopped and walked with the fearful cottony steps I had taken in Harlem, in a million places, toward the flames. I don't know whether people scattered, but if some did, it would make perfect sense. I stayed for a while. And then I came back the next day. And I came back every day for about a month, from sunrise until as late as I could stand it.

It was winter, and people were trying to survive by huddling around a fire that they had made in a barrel. There was massive distrust for the first week or so after I arrived. And there was some sort of breakthrough when I pooled money and went to the place on the corner that sold cigarettes and beer. I bought two forty-ounce bottles of malt liquor. Several days of that, and the trust factor went higher. I thought after a while of how easy it would be to become an alcoholic. After a while, I was almost deadened, inured, to the mad spikes. One day some knives were pulled and people squared off, and I didn't move, didn't seem par-

ticularly alarmed. It was as if it were happening on the outer edges of the frame. I went home very late at night, and my wife said my entire body smelled like smoke. I felt as though I had been inside a house that was burning. As always, I thought a lot about the fact that when our little ensemble splintered for the evening—the Texas writer A. C. Greene wrote me a note saying that he thought my story was like a play—most of the actors walked into the alleys or went to the bus stop, whereas I got in my car and went to a house with a refrigerator that was fairly full.

For an evanescent second, faces in the cars gliding by on the South Dallas boulevard on their way to Fair Park, to the highway, to anywhere else instinctively turn toward . . . something.

It is something behind a crumbling wall, the last real remnant of a brick building. Something just through the doorway. Something just a few steps beyond this falling portal. Flames like fat, capricious horsetails. Webs of smoke. Ebbing wisps of laughter. A jumble of bodies. The shimmering blink of matches catching spark. The hiss of wood being turned to ash.

It is all around the barrel. The barrel with the fire inside. The fire that must be fed and served. Nothing is more important to the soul of this place they call The Hole.

"It's the center of everything," offers sweet-faced Verta Ivy, thirty-seven, as she stares away from me and into the roiling barrel. "It's like something in a church."

She is here, like the others, almost every day near the intersection of Oakland Avenue and Martin Luther King, Jr. Boulevard. Some come for just a few minutes a day. Some arrive at six in the morning and stay until the sun rises again. It is a community with a specific chorus: A tall salesman with a blue suit and black briefcase. Two lovers—the sixty-two-year-old man leans on one wooden crutch, his thirty-two-year-old companion carries a dull knife and swears she will use it. A wide-eyed concrete worker who served in a four-man killing squad in Vietnam. A round woman named Baby Rabbit. A splendidly dressed man called Cash. A childlike person known as Lightning. A middle-school student. An infant staring through the bars of a shopping cart. A roofer with shoes drenched in tar. A hopeful plumber clutching his bag of tools. A slender homeless man who wants custody of his four children and dreams of being an astronaut. The most controversial city council member in Texas. Someone who simply slumps into the folds of an old abandoned couch.

They are the shifting constants, the ones dutifully assembling—even in the blistering summer and numbing winter—every day for decades. They are the ones who come here searching for work. For dialogue. For companionship. For simple warmth. For protection. For food, for money, for a drink, for a game of dominoes.

"The Hole is reality," swears Verta's husband, Eddie Ervin. He is a fifty-seven-year-old Vietnam veteran who has his crumbling honorable-discharge papers stuffed into his pockets. He is warning me, and maybe he is telling me he already sees through me. "You don't know a damn thing about The Hole. You don't know nothing about The Hole until you have to come here every day of your life."

Everyone in The Hole is looking for a thing he or she rarely attains. Every day, several step through the portal and hope someone will come by to "catch them"—to hire them—for day labor. If they get picked, they've gotten what is called "catch-out." For years, people have known that crew bosses come to The Hole searching for quick, cheap help. It could be a carpenter, a landscaper, a mason, a trash hauler, a bricklayer, or a roofer who parks his pickup truck near The Hole. Sometimes the boss comes in himself. Most of the time, because he is very afraid, he sends someone else into The Hole.

They want to rent bodies for a few hours. A warm body to work with hot tar, yards of bubbling concrete, acres of rotting garbage. They want someone to work for less than minimum wage. Someone who will take a chance on a check that might not clear. Someone who might never see a single dollar for breaking his back. Catch-out is a deep, withering part of life in The Hole. It is a way of survival, and it binds the men, women, and children who pass their days and nights there, all of them stepping up to the rotting metal barrel that is filled with blazing trash, wood, and paper. And virtually around the clock each winter day, dozens of people come to stand by the fire, to feed the fire, to scavenge for anything—twigs, old furniture, rags, oily garbage bags—that can be set afire inside the barrel. It is, of course, eternal, and people fight desperately to keep the flames alive.

At five thirty in the morning, I'm standing in The Hole with Bobby White. He has come to The Hole with a sixty-dollar money order in his pocket and lines on his face from being up for days on end. Bobby White knows how to greet the dawn. He has spent a decade as a plumber's helper. The last time he had some catch-out, he was even able to get a second day of work, but only after he caught a bus from South Dallas, traveled to Balch Springs, and waited there for the boss to pick him up.

The forty-six-year-old tells me he once lived in Kansas City but moved back to Texas when his parents died. In the early 1980s, when Dallas's prospects seemed as long as a limousine, Bobby White was "the man"—he would come to The Hole and hire his own crews. Now it has been weeks since anybody has come for him. It is drizzling, and he stamps his feet against the predawn cold, hangs onto his bag of work clothes, and casts hopeful glances when he hears footsteps approaching.

Uncle Joe is also here, his fingernails and boots coated with sealants and the 600-degree tar he has poured all over Dallas: "Mary Kay Cosmetics. Public library. Reunion Arena. LTV. Schools in Arlington. In Grand Prairie. Thanksgiving Square. Wadley Blood Bank," chants Uncle Joe. His nephew, Smokey Jackson, thirty-eight, is listening and occasionally flicking fat fire-barrel ashes off his thick glasses. Smokey has the same black fingernails, the same burn scars up and down his arms. He is in the middle of a big roofing job at the Freedom Baptist Church in Oak Cliff. Because it is raining and he can't work, he has gone to The Hole.

"I come here every day when I don't work," says Smokey, who lives, like his uncle, in Oak Cliff. He argues that a roofer "makes more than an average executive, but he just doesn't bank it." Smokey has boiled things down to this: "I can't afford to sit around and worry. When I get my money, I pay my bills. When I work, I work."

Ernest Smith, sixty-five, and known to everyone as Mr. Dick, has been in The Hole since he left his nearby home before seven. He makes ends meet with odd jobs, and he wants the catch-out crew to know it. I saw him come through the portal as the sun came up, pushing a green plastic cart filled with his collection of aluminum cans. On the outside, in big letters, he has painted "MR. DICK." On the inside, he has a boom box cranked up and playing B. B. King sermons. He used to drive a forklift, has been married five times, and says he owns fourteen tailor-made suits and ninety pairs of shoes. On the coldest days, he has the warmest clothing in The Hole. "I haven't bought a store-made suit since the time my daddy died," Mr. Dick announces to us.

To one side of The Hole, a man named Smitty has brought along two Goodyear Eagle tires and a plastic bucket with one brush and one sponge. He tells me he wants fifteen dollars each for the tires and a dollar for the bucket and its contents.

Eddie Ervin knows that Smitty will never get what he wants. He believes that people in The Hole rarely get anything they want. "It's a suicide mission. It's a fake deal. They're using us. It's not with whips, chains, and bull-dogs anymore," he begins, as he waves his hands toward the warmth of the fire. "Man, this is survival. This is the only way. You have to bow down and do things you wouldn't normally do."

By now, he is shouting. We are watching him carefully. Eddie, who has made as much as $110 a day doing catch-out concrete work, springs to his feet. He hasn't had catch-out in weeks. His wife, Verta, brings home $276 every two weeks by working in a nursing home. They get $236 in food stamps and their rent is $310 a month. "You know where you really get fucked?" he demands as he shoves one of his sleeves as far up his arm as it will go.

"Right here," he says to me, pointing to his black skin.

O n the tiny garage that borders The Hole, someone who can't spell has written, in pencil: "By love you no who you are." It is signed "Court-ney." Nearby is a fistful of plastic roses attached to some ominous-looking electrical wires. The city council member says he knows whom Courtney was writing about. Al Lipscomb was last here a few weeks ago, though this isn't his district. He grew up in the area; his relatives are still nearby. He says The Hole and the people in it are not far removed from his world. Not very far away from anybody's world.

"I was there three weeks ago. I come through, and people say they knew me when—when we all used to put in together for peanut butter and bolo-gna sandwiches," remembers Lipscomb. Lingering, sitting, and watching, he felt enveloped by equal doses of anger and sadness. "You know how when you see people on the highway with signs asking for food and you hope you don't make eye contact? It's the same thing when people pass by [The Hole]," he tells me.

"You go through there, and you get a very embittered view. They've just about given up. This is what is so tragic. I think some of the guys are coming under the pretense of catch-out, but it's not there. They pitch in for some wine to pass the day away. It's a little country club."

A Texas country club with enormous dues: "It just erodes the soul," he says to me one bitterly cold day when he glides into The Hole.

L arry Franklin, tall, smart, and intense—and in The Hole every day—can talk about erosion, about souls, about "dreams and goals." But country clubs might be the furthest thing from his mind. One frigid morning, the forty-seven-year-old slips another cigarette into his mouth and spells it out. He grew up in Dallas, went to Lincoln High, then to El Centro Community College, and now he has been getting temporary minimum-wage factory jobs. "These people hire us so they don't have to hire anyone permanently.

I've got goals. The goal is money. It's security. Can you pay the rent? Pay your utilities? Feed your family?"

He drags on his cigarette, and a cloud of smoke frames the scowl on his face. Linger in The Hole, and your whole body smells like a fire, like smoke, like the charred remains of a house that burned down only a short time ago. The wind cuts through the alleys, through the abandoned doorways of the old businesses, and it makes the fire in the barrel roar and leap. It seems to reach up and take aim at a particular person now and then, bathing that person in smoke, ash, and smell. Spend a day, a night in The Hole and the fire in the barrel will find you. It happens to everyone.

Larry knows. The Hole, he says, is all about the elemental things in life: jobs, escape, and warmth on a day as cold as death. "That's all The Hole is," insists Larry, a stabbing edge to his voice. I assume he thinks I'm lost, really lost, on some stupid-ass search for meaning. His anger seems to coil through his body.

"This ain't no chess match. It's nothing that complicated."

After Verta Ivy clocks out at her nursing-home job, she comes to The Hole to free her mind. To be with her personal and extended family. She wants to believe love holds people in The Hole together. Today she has brought along her thirteen-year-old son, David. "This is my testimony whenever I get in church. This is my miracle," she coos as she lovingly lays a large hand on David's head and brings him closer to the fire. "I'd walk a muddy river for him."

For twenty-two days, David was laid up in Children's Medical Center as an infection ate away his muscle tissue. In The Hole, he lifts his shirt to show me an endless, awful parade of thick jagged scars up and down his body. "He holds a lot inside him," says Verta, cradling her son's head in her arms. David, embarrassed by the attention, seems more absorbed by the rattle and hum inside The Hole. Mother and son draw even closer to the fire barrel. Sometimes Verta goes to other, smaller holes in South Dallas. She calls it "hole hopping." But she always comes back to this one. She is secure here.

Freddy Edwards knows how Verta feels. She is forty-four and a ranking member of The Hole for ten years. It is, she quietly admits to me, her family. She lives with her boyfriend ("he's an older man") in a $300-a-month apartment on South Boulevard. She cares for two grandchildren—Lakwanna, six, and Tiffany, seven—and gets $90 a month in disability support for both of them. She brings home $591 a month in food stamps and federal aid. "I love everybody up here. We're like brothers and sisters," she allows. She sometimes brings her grandchildren to The Hole. "I was intending to bring them up here yesterday. They know to find me here."

Carolyn Hester, bony and intense, is sitting on a tree stump off to one side of The Hole. Her eyes are darting as she negotiates her way through a nagging swirl of paperwork. The Hole is a place to tread through job applications, welfare requests, homework sheets, insurance papers, legal documents, and a thundering herd of other forms handed out by the various agencies inside the nearby Martin Luther King, Jr. Community Center. Carolyn fidgets and stares down at the official-looking letters in her long fingers. They indicate that the food stamp people want $203 back from her. She normally gets $253 a month in stamps. One section of the letter talks about setting up a repayment plan.

She stares at the papers for a long, long time and asks me to interpret them for her. Even after weeks in The Hole, I don't know what to say to her. I squat down close to her and stare at the papers. They seem like pages that are empty of any logic. They contain numbers and words stacked in some inscrutable language and pattern. She is watching me. I don't want to hold the papers. I want to say the right thing—anything, really. And we look at each other as if we are always going to be the most distant of strangers.

Bobby White saved Eddie Truitt's life last night.

A big man, a bouncer, had Eddie around the neck in the alley at the back of The Hole. An argument had erupted, things got loud, and finally Bobby White stuck his hand in the middle of things. The big man dropped Eddie like a sack of wet cement. For a long moment Eddie didn't move: "He's knocking at the gate," someone yelled.

The next day, Eddie leaves his falling-down shack in Oak Cliff, across the way from the packinghouse ("Home of Oink Sausage," it says out front), and takes long, purposeful strides down 11th Street. He hooks a turn and begins the miles-long march across the narrow, low-lying bridge over the Trinity River and toward The Hole. This day, by the time he finally arrives at nine, The Hole is gurgling, the fire is blazing.

Bobby White is there, sunglasses on his face, workbag in his hand. Pinetop, who is retired and "living on checks from Uncle Sam," is here, putting his full weight on the one crutch he carries. And all morning, much to Eddie's exasperation, the people in The Hole are breaking him. Busting Eddie verbally. Jabbing unmercifully at him. They insist he would be dead if his friends in The Hole didn't love him. If strangers to The Hole weren't challenged. If they didn't have to pass tests of time before they were accepted at The Hole. If—bottom line—loyalty and family didn't count for a lot. As I listen, I am laughing too, looking through the shifting smoke, trying to make the faces out, trying to see who is here.

It is seven in the morning, a few minutes before Lightning is ready to go to The Hole. I watch him tug his raggedy red and brown blankets tighter around his bony body. Icy water has been thudding through the cracks in the ceiling all night. Puddles are forming on the edge of the ratty mattress he found. The quiet, reed-thin and angular-faced twenty-eight-year-old—his real name is Andrew Alexander—has been living in an abandoned garage behind a lawyer's office on Martin Luther King, Jr. Boulevard for eighteen months.

Last night, when Lightning returned from The Hole, he learned he had been cleaned out. Cleaned out of fifteen dollars' worth of food he had been able to assemble because of catch-out. That fifteen dollars, earned because someone had come looking for a guy to do a day's yard work in Duncanville, was his only bit of catch-out all week long.

With his cash, Lightning did what he always did. He walked with his mutt, Candy, down to the Gold Star grocery. He reminded the manager again that he wanted work at the grocery, cleaning up the broken bottles and trash in the parking lot. Lightning, who went through the ninth grade at Lincoln High, bought dog food, canned fish, canned beans. He had fifty cents left over, and he treated himself to one gold-colored can of Olde English malt liquor. He hid his food in his garage home and went to The Hole. When he returned, everything that he had was gone, except for one small white-labeled can of spinach.

Now, as he sits in The Hole, he tells me he is weighing a midafternoon run to a Dumpster behind a fried-chicken place. On a good day, he can get six half-eaten breasts for himself and a bunch of parts for Candy. If he is lucky, there will be a biscuit. He is also thinking about going to an alley near Colonial and Martin Luther King, Jr. Boulevard. He wants an ID—it will help him get a job—and you can buy them there for three dollars.

All day, Lightning has been pacing and wearing his pain like a badge. The people in The Hole know he usually isn't like that. He is the first to find wood and cardboard for the fire barrel, the last to ask for anything. But now, in The Hole, the weight of the theft seems to be pressing on his shoulders. He looks as if he is sinking into his soiled green jacket. He stoops to grab a piece of paper blowing through the ashes, wine bottles, and dirt.

He presses the grimy paper to the tears streaming down his face.

The Hole has grown quiet.

"People shouldn't do you like that," he manages to say before he turns his head away from us.

It is the day Ollison Presley, Jr., is being laid down. It is the day Ollison Presley, Jr., is being dispatched to his version of Valhalla. And those who knew him are gathering in The Hole. Gathering and unraveling his legacy.

Round-faced Hubert Chandler, who was just let go from his job operating a loader, has come. Donnie "The Truth" Truitt, with the hand-carved walking sticks he wants to sell to the white kids in Deep Ellum. And Jimmy "They Call Me Cash" Priest is also here, the sun slicing through the wickedly cold air and making the silver threads in his suit shine like little metal bars. He clutches a rumpled piece of amber-colored paper. It is the notice he has brought back from the Golden Gate Funeral Home, the stately place in Oak Cliff where the biggest mansions in Dallas used to stand.

Those at the funeral insist that Ollison, who was blown away after he raised a knife outside The Hole, near a joint called The Cape, never looked finer. They swear that, lying in his open casket, the forty-year-old appeared to be floating on a sea of pastels. Appeared to be going to his great reward on a soothing blanket of dreams. In The Hole, people stare down at the words written in Ollison Presley, Jr.'s funeral notice: "He united with the church at an early age . . . and attended public schools in Dallas, Texas."

And a few are huddling, muttering that Presley "brought his death on himself."

Eddie Ervin puts it this way to me: "You didn't have to kill him, because you knew somebody was going to kill him for you."

Around us, around the fire barrel, people solemnly nod their heads. But some people in The Hole also know that Ollison Presley, Jr., passed this way looking to catch out on his specialty, paint and bodywork. Ollison Presley, Jr., passed through The Hole, and that stood for something. He came here for many of the same jumbled reasons that drove everybody else to the fire barrel in the goddamned dead of winter in Texas.

"When one of us leaves, if I have to wear short pants, I'll be there at the funeral," trumpets Cash. He likes to say he is a "jack of all trades, master of none." He does concrete finishing and works part time at the Packing House Market. "I don't care. I'll go to the church and ask them to give me a suit to wear. I'll be there when one of us leaves."

I have been in The Hole for weeks. I know that once I stop coming, I will never come back.

Pinetop's wife—he is sixty-two and she is thirty-two—has a thin-bladed knife in her fist, and she wants to shove it just below Freddy Edwards's breasts. She has taken offense at something Freddy has said.

Pinetop is knocked to the ground. People in The Hole drift to the corners. I watch as a few struggle to separate the women. Freddy and Pinetop's wife both flee—each heading in a different direction. Pinetop watches them and slumps onto the old couch next to the fire barrel. He is rumpled, and his forehead is covered with sweat.

Things mutate in a sliver of a second in The Hole, in the same fraction of time that Ollison Presley, Jr., lost his life only a few yards away. Someone drinks too much. Someone smokes crack. Someone's patience splinters. There are arguments every day. But still, the police rarely visit The Hole, unless someone's blood is shed.

Arvell J. Dugas saw his blood on his own hands just a few weeks ago. Someone smashed him in the head with a forty-ounce bottle of Crazy Horse malt liquor. He spent two weeks at Parkland Memorial Hospital undergoing speech therapy. Today he is wheeling his rusty shopping cart into The Hole. Almost everything that is important to him is inside. There are important papers in a King Edward cigar box. Important telephone numbers shoehorned into the tiny margins of a pocket-sized version of the New Testament. Notes pertaining to his four young children and their mother, who are in California. Phone numbers, addresses, correspondence. But things have been unsettled, even more than usual, since he was attacked.

"I don't care who sends me to space, I'll thank God for getting me there," Arvell tells me as he gingerly hand-rolls a Bugler cigarette.

The thirty-two-year-old spent six years in the navy. He wants to be an astronaut. But for now, he spends his time moving from one abandoned house, or "armadillo hole," to another. Arvell is living on $112 a month in food stamps. And until he sees his children, until he travels to outer space, he whispers that he has learned to look for God. To look for God even in The Hole.

"I keep praying to God to give me guidance," he says, staring straight ahead.

While Arvell has been talking, Pinetop has been trying to piece himself back together, to catch his breath, after the women's scuffle. He says that he, too, sometimes wishes everything were different. People are gathering wood for the barrel—even strangers like me, people who don't live anywhere nearby, have learned to keep the fire alive. I sprint down the alley, back where the garbage trucks are supposed to pick up trash, and dig through weeds, through mounds of refuse, looking for anything flammable. It is what you do in The Hole. If you don't feed the fire, then why you are there? The cold is numbing, creeping. The cold is endless, everywhere, and the fire is all that matters to me.

Pinetop runs his hands over his secondhand coat.

"We're all wearing dead folks' clothes," he laughs.

"I'll get on my knees and make concrete," Eddie Ervin blurts out. It is an icy Saturday afternoon. Ervin's last catch-out came when a man hired him to go north to Plano Road and work on a driveway. When they were through, he gave Eddie ten dollars and told him to wait at the bus station near The Hole for the other eighty. Eddie and his wife sat for an hour. Two hours. Three hours. The police drove by. And finally Eddie went back into The Hole, the anger welling up inside.

Now he is standing inches away from the roaring blaze inside the barrel. I helped tear up the last few boards in an old couch to feed the flames. Waves of heat are wrapping around the barrel, making it seem to move, making it seem alive. Eddie is thinking about Vietnam, about life in The Hole, about a lifetime of having to go to the barrel because it is there—because there really is no other place to go.

"If you can't survive one way, you survive another way. That's what it's all about. The barrel with the fire in it? It's all about staying alive."

The Hole is gone. The portal to The Hole was eventually knocked down, and any intimation of a closed world was destroyed. City planners say there are plans to turn the area where The Hole existed into a bus depot. The people in The Hole found other places to gather around a fire barrel, and in the twenty-first century, you can easily find, in winter, the wisps of flame back behind other crumbling buildings, in other dirt-paved alleys in South Dallas.

SOUTH DALLAS BLUES

Dallas was overheated, dizzy with fear and accusations. There had been people shooting at cops, and cops shooting at citizens. Dallas had always been able to put a lid on overt racial tension—some smart observers had called it "the accommodation." The power players in the city had essentially purchased peace; they had gone to black church leaders and offered them money and support to work harder to make sure that people and plans didn't coalesce. That the streets didn't erupt.

We heard that the downtown McDonald's had begun blasting classical music to drive away the kids who were hanging out. Most of the kids seemed to be African American. It was at some bizarre stage. We decided to do a story about searching for common ground. One reporter was asked to follow the cops, to take to the streets with them and ride around. I was told to talk to the people, the ones who felt they were on the receiving end of whatever it was the cops were dealing. Late one night on Martin Luther King, Jr. Boulevard, I saw a swirl of police lights at a cheap motel. I stopped to see what was going on. The other reporter was there. The cops, most of whom seemed to be white, were after someone. It didn't really seem, from what we could tell, that common ground was in sight. We were out on a street that some people liked to think had once been named after the Confederate general who helped found the KKK. And one family would only talk to me from behind the bars on their front door.

Hudson Griffin tells me he likes the cops. Always has. He is sitting in the little work lair of his tailoring and cleaning shop on Oakland Avenue. The sun is falling down Pine Street, and light slices through his burglar bars.

It makes patterns on the clothing Griffin is hunching over. His rugged hands nimbly guide a needle through a pair of tan pants.

"I don't have any trouble with the police," says Griffin, smiling down at his handiwork. "They're part of the neighborhood just like anything else."

From the back of Griffin's timeworn store, a radio voice is filtering through the racks of dry cleaning: *police report a shooting in South Dallas . . .*

Griffin looks up from the alteration, one of thousands he has done since he began work in South Dallas in the 1940s. The radio tells us that police have shot a suspected prostitute after a chase into an apartment complex.

"There you go," he tells me, bursting into laughter.

"Now, is that what you're looking for?"

Griffin and the people who live and work in South Dallas grow tired of strangers like me showing up in the neighborhood, the ones who come and go as if we were unearthing clues to an alien civilization. Lately, we have been out and about more often. The police killed elderly Etta Collins on Metropolitan Avenue: before the week was out, her death had kicked the relationship between the cops and the South Dallas neighborhoods back into the thorny realm of "issues." With it came editorials, analyses, inquiries. There were meetings at Madison High School and St. Luke Community United Methodist Church and talk of a congressional hearing. "It's frustrating, it's frustrating, it's frustrating," says Griffin. "The big fish is always eating the little fish. The people without clout are always the ones to finish last. We don't want attention. We just want to be treated fairly and to live fairly."

Anyone who has spent any time walking the seven main arteries of South Dallas—Grand, Martin Luther King, Hatcher, Lagow, Robert B. Cullum, Second Avenue, Bexar—knows the regal Hudson Griffin. Some people call him the mayor of South Dallas. He has been on the front lines with the NAACP for decades. People on Oakland know Griffin and they know his frustration. They have seen naïve reporters come and go. Seen police come and go. Seen businesses come and go. Seen politicians make once-only visits to the powerful preachers and leading businessmen.

"People talk about the problem down in South Dallas," Griffin tells me. "Go to Boston, go to St. Louis, go to Chicago. They've got problems. I know we have problems, too, but I like it here. I was born and raised here. Many folks come to Dallas and they're told to stay away from South Dallas. People put labels on things."

It is not hard to find people who are clearly aware they live in a part of town too often captured by catchwords and instant assessments: Poverty. Crime. A community "accommodated." A place of white flight. The place where racially motivated bombings took place in the 1950s. "Task forces" are mobilized to tackle South Dallas as if it were a marauding, diseased part of the city. There have been and still are too many times when the bond between South Dallas and the most visible city servants—the police—is broken. People are suspicious that double standards exist within the police department: one set of rules for Dallas, and another set for South Dallas.

"I like the police. We need the police. He's supposed to be your friend," insists Griffin to me as customers drift into his store. The tailor puts down the pants he is mending. "But I'll tell you this," he says, "a black person in Dallas never knows what's going to happen when the police stop you." Inside Griffin's establishment, his customers nod in silent agreement. It is quiet; it is time for me to leave. A short walk away is Oakland Cemetery, where Confederate general Robert Gano is buried. I wonder whether Griffin knows that Howard Hughes was directly related to Gano.

Sidney "Bo" Johns wants his title duly noted: recording secretary and assistant financial secretary, Park South YMCA Senior Men's Domino Club.

"Got all that?" he asks me, speaking through a cloud of cigarette smoke.

Johns is a retired postal clerk and an intimidating domino player. He is handsome, tall, sophisticated-looking in a turtleneck shirt. His friends say he is mellow, predictable, still looking after his mother down on Coolidge Street. Johns dislikes the police. He has for half a century.

In 1936, the Texas Centennial was uncorking at Fair Park. There wouldn't be blacks on the police force until the 1940s. Johns was walking on Second Avenue. He had a job delivering the *Dallas Dispatch*, and he was hurrying to pick up papers. Without warning, two policemen jumped out of a car and ran at him with pistols drawn. He was kicked in the ribs, punched in the head. The police shoved him back and forth. When they drove away, without Johns ever knowing why they had stopped, the teenager staggered home. Confused and scared, he never told his father, a chauffeur, or his mother, a maid. "I finally got around to telling my mother about ten years ago," says Johns.

His mother's response: "I told you so."

When Johns was young, he listened to stories about the police. He heard them at the only high school for blacks, Booker T. Washington. Johns's teachers had warned the students to be wary of the police. The police could rob a man of his pride. "People grew up in Dallas thinking that the Ku Klux Klan was headquartered in the police department," offers Johns.

The year after Johns was mugged by the police, he was working part time as a doorman at The Century Backyard nightclub at Metropolitan and Octavia. A woman was hit in the head by a stranger lurking in the parking lot. The police took Johns downtown even though he insisted he didn't know who did it. He spent the night in jail. He had even more to think about, including the fact that he saw police beating the hell out of people in a nearby cell.

"My mother wanted me to leave Dallas. You know how mothers are. She knew the way things were for young blacks," remembers Johns. He had transferred to the new Lincoln High School and played football. But by 1942, at the urging of his mother, Johns left for San Francisco; he had heard they were hiring welders in the shipyards. He wound up working for the postal service; in 1967, he transferred to South Dallas to care for his mother.

Things hadn't changed.

His first week back, his car was stopped, along with hundreds of others, in a sweeping police check near Oakland Avenue. "OK, boy, just watch your step," the policeman said. He flicked Johns's license in his face. Johns pinched back his anger. Twenty years later, Johns's face tightens as he tells the story: "I had to hold myself back. I thought that was one of the reasons she [his mother] sent me away. She was afraid I would get killed. I would have. I was very hot tempered."

Johns kept his cool, though there were other close encounters. The police confronted him while he was fishing around in the trunk of his Corvair. The tones were accusatory. Johns bristled. "You people don't appreciate anything anyone does for you," snarled the policeman.

A few years ago, the police pulled Johns over and accused him of speeding. When he reached for the license tucked in his visor, he looked up to find another policeman at his passenger-side window. The officer was squared off and aiming his revolver at Johns's face. "I thought I was dead. I had my heart in my mouth."

Johns is almost resigned when he tells me about the incidents. The police are, for Johns, pieces of a lingering cancer. "I had a friend who went up to North Dallas, and they charged him thirty-two dollars for a drink because he was black. What are you going to do?" I don't know what to tell him.

Johns says he knows exactly what he'll do. Stay in South Dallas in his $203-a-month apartment. Keep attending Mt. Carmel Baptist Church on Metropolitan Avenue. Assume his domino duties at ten thirty every morning. He also knows that he has given up trying to figure out why the police treated him the way they did: "I don't think I'll ever understand it. That's the price you pay for being black." He smiles at me and laughs as he raises his thumb, sticks out his index finger, and pretends he is shooting a gun.

Falicia Anderson and her sister, Shebaa Green, are locking themselves in for the night. They live in a small apartment just off South Boulevard in what was once one of the most exclusive areas of Texas. Two blocks to the west there are still fine, sprawling two-story homes on both sides of the street. On the sisters' side of South Boulevard there are row after row of apartment complexes. Their narrow three-room place costs $265 a month. There is no phone. They turn the oven on to warm the place.

"Have you ever heard the South Dallas theme song?" Green asks me. They study my face and giggle conspiratorially. She begins imitating a police siren and then collapses in laughter.

"Everyone thinks South Dallas is so bad," she says. "They think people are shooting each other. They think the police are shooting people. It's not like that. I think South Dallas is like anyplace else. There are certain parts of South Dallas you just stay away from."

The sisters are both single parents. Their days, their lives in South Dallas, revolve around Green's three-year-old daughter, LaShebaa, and Anderson's one-year-old daughter, LaDonna. At six thirty in the morning, the women are bustling around the apartment. Green is in her blue Lone Star Gas uniform. The children are ready to be dropped off at their day-care centers: LaDonna goes to the Warren Avenue Baptist Church, LaShebaa to the Mt. Olive Lutheran Church. The sisters moved to South Dallas so they could be close to day care, and because they thought South Dallas was safer than the Oak Cliff neighborhood they grew up in. If Green has time, she drives her sister to her maintenance job at the Dallas Museum of Art. If she is in a hurry to get to her job as a service technician for the gas company, her sister takes the bus. By six in the evening they have picked up their daughters and are back at the small apartment. Green turns on the radio, moves to the kitchen, and begins heating some red beans and rice. "One thing the police need to do is stop for you more often. They'll see you out there hurting, and they'll just cruise by," she says. "They can stop more often and see if people need help instead of just riding past."

LaDonna squirms in her mother's lap. LaShebaa does an impromptu dance to the music. Their parents watch them. For the most part, the sisters keep to themselves. They are homebodies. You won't find them at Club 97,

The Arandas Club, or Lat's Panache. They eat at home, not at Yvonne's, or Lim's Cafeteria, or Meshack's Barbeque. If they go to a movie—there are no cinemas in their neighborhood—it is to the dollar show at the Texas Theater in Oak Cliff.

The children are everything.

"Everyone heard about the old lady who was killed. Those things happen. The police have a job to do," Anderson tells me. "I wouldn't hesitate to call the police. That's what they are there for. The police are all you really have to protect your family." When I leave, they carefully lock the bars on their door. I see them staring at me as I walk down the street.

The historical marker at the end of Leo Chaney, Jr.'s stretch of block is testimony to the fact that Dallas's prominent Jews once lived on South Boulevard. Now, the large two-story homes, nestled under towering oak trees and set far back from the street, are owned by blacks. Chaney's father, well known in South Dallas for his cleaners and washaterias on Grand and Spring avenues, has lived on the block for almost thirty years. Chaney Jr., his wife, Phyliss, and their three children have lived across the street for the last three years.

"Our family goes way back in South Dallas," says Chaney Jr. "My father lived in Frazier Courts [a housing project to the east]. I went to Madison High School. I always knew that I would live in South Dallas. My sons are going to live here, too." Chaney and his wife are settling into lounge chairs, their backs to a massive fireplace set into a far wall of their sixty-year-old brick home. It is Saturday evening. Their children and kids from the neighborhood are bounding from one room to another. Outside, the old-fashioned street lamps are beginning to flicker with light.

Two years ago, he and his wife were driving down Central Expressway. Dressed in a suit and tie, driving a new car, Chaney exited the freeway and found a policeman signaling him to pull over. He did, and as he reached for the door handle, he saw the policeman reach for his gun. "I said, 'Wait a minute, partner. What's going on here?' Here I was. I've got an education. I've got a little bit of money. I'm dressed right. I'm in my new car. And I'm about to get shot."

His wife shakes her head as she listens to her husband. She admonishes him for not mentioning that the policeman also called her husband "boy." "We can't live without the police," she tells me. "We must have them. I think if we just saw them more often, if they were around more often, we wouldn't have problems with them."

Last October, the day after her birthday, she was robbed in her driveway after coming home one evening from shopping. "I realized that the only time you see the police is after the fact. I don't ever see them," she says. Their youngest son, Paul, has settled into his mother's lap. In a back room, his two brothers are yelling and running. Periodically, their father raises his voice a few notches and asks them to quiet down. "I expect my children to grow up to be respectful of the police. I want them to be lawful. I also don't want them to grow up with prejudices. I'm not going to hand down to them bad feelings about the police," says Chaney. "But I also want my children to retain their dignity. This is America. South Dallas, Texas, is in the United States of America."

Snake and Head have hit the highway down the block from Snake's house on Metropolitan Avenue. In Snake's Cutlass, they pass by the big sign hanging over Central Expressway: "Change your life . . . call college." It's early Tuesday morning, and there are people strolling past the Kirkwood CME Temple on Octavia. Snake needs money to put a shock absorber on his Cutlass. He is on his way to Pleasant Grove to borrow twenty dollars.

Snake's real name is John Wayne Snow. People have called him Snake for years. He has it written on his high-top basketball sneakers. Head's real name is Derrick Richardson. People have called him Head a long time, but the name took on extra poignancy late last year. Head says he woke in the night with flames eating away at his face, hands, chest. Someone threw gasoline on him and followed up with a match. He says he knows who did it but that the police are still investigating. One side of his face is scarred, his arms are bound in bandages, patches of his hair are missing.

People never believe Snake is thirty-four. He looks younger than the eighteen-year-old Head. They are best friends and running buddies. They also know South Dallas better than anyone.

"There are some parts of Bexar Street where you do only one thing," laughs Snake.

He is in the slow lane on the Hawn Freeway, passing over Bexar Street. To the south are the Rhoads Terrace projects; the main street winding through the housing projects is called Tuxedo Drive.

"Run or die," replies Head.

They both cackle and continue driving toward Pleasant Grove. Snake and Head know about running. They figured out the hassle factor long ago. Stay in motion, stay off Oakland, stay off Bexar, and your chances of being stopped by the police plummet. "If the police just see you hanging out," Snake tells me, "they automatically think you're up to something."

Head is thinking about pursuing a job with Kentucky Fried Chicken. Snake puts in weekends with the army reserve and collects a monthly check. Both do occasional chores at the Park South YMCA. Head lives with friends in a big house off Pennsylvania, the roar of the highway forever thundering through the wooden frame. He walks the five blocks to Snake's place, a comfortable home owned by Snake's mother. On the way, every day, he passes dozens of men his age and older. They hang out by the private clubs on Grand and abandoned buildings on Pennsylvania. In the winter, in the empty lots feeding off the highway, they light fires inside trash bins and sit on discarded chairs. The fireplace and furniture are there on a slab where they hang out. The only thing missing is a house.

Nine people live at Snake's, including Snake's cousin Butch. After Snake and Head pick up a shock absorber—a friend gave them the twenty-dollar loan—they return to the house. Butch sits on the porch and watches them work on the car. "The lawman is crooked," claims Butch. "I've seen the lawman take a pinch out of a pack of pot. I've seen cops in uniform throwing dice in crap games. You think people in South Dallas don't think the lawman has a secret graveyard?" By now, I think he is right.

Snake looks up from under the car and smiles at me. He recalls being stuck in traffic on Second Avenue, waiting for a funeral procession to roll on. At Reed Lane, he peeled off, turned right, and headed west. A police car appeared in his rearview mirror. Snake followed the curves, passing the old Confederate cemetery centered in the heart of South Dallas. Finally, the police lights went on. Snake pulled over. The policeman said he was speeding. Snake denied it. The policeman took him downtown for having too heavily tinted windows, a suspended license, and no insurance. He spent two weeks in jail and was told to pay fines.

"If you're young and you're in a car, they'll get you every time," says Head. "The less you have to do with the police, the better. If somebody breaks into a house, you think it's going to do any good to call the police? Forget it. Your stuff is gone. You'll see somebody else wearing it."

It is pushing two in the afternoon, and Snake scrambles out from under his Cutlass. He and Head drive off to begin their daily ritual: playing basketball until nine. They turn toward Exline Street. They are in a hurry. By midafternoon on any weekday, the gym is packed with dozens of men, many of them in their twenties, playing the best basketball in Texas.

Two blocks from the center, Snake and Head pass a black teenager spread-eagle with his hands on the hood of a car. Three policemen are gathered around him, writing and somberly talking to each other. Snake chuckles.

One of the policemen is the same one who arrested him.

"Well, well, it's a small world after all," says Snake.

Marilynn Mayse lost her mind the day she came home and found that her house had been broken into—again. It had been only two years since she had scrubbed the walls, feverishly trying to sanitize the place, to make it clean, after her sister was raped at gunpoint. The rapist had come in at night; he didn't leave until the morning. When he walked out the door, he turned to her sister and said: "Lock your door, you don't want people breaking in."

There had been three other break-ins, including the time they took her high school ring and clothing. They came at night. They came in broad daylight. They pried the doors open. Once they just kicked them down. But when they stole Marilynn Mayse's air conditioners in the dead of summer, she snapped. She ran out the front door and into the street. Yelling at anyone she saw. Crying and cursing. She ran to the apartment complexes at the end of the block. She screamed: "You people are not men. You're boys. You just sit and watch people steal from women." The neighbors watched her for a while from behind their screen doors and then drifted away.

"I had been away, in Atlanta, and it was just the last thing in the world I wanted to have happen," she tells me.

It is eight o'clock on a Friday night, and her friends have grown accustomed to not seeing her. Each day after working at the Dallas County Community Corrections Department, she is back home. She graduated from law school at the University of Texas, and now the bar exam is looming. There are books, papers, and pens piled in different corners.

"What I want is for the cops to drive down my street. I'm being held hostage in my own house. I don't want to stay on guard all the time. I've got burglar alarms. I've got burglar bars. I need police in my neighborhood. They have never done anything to me but maybe hurt my feelings. I'm not afraid that the cops will shoot me. It's the dopeheads that will shoot me."

She likes South Dallas. Something drew her back to her old neighborhood. She likes the fact that she was able to buy a house on the same block that she grew up on: her mother lives two doors down in the home she has had for thirty-four years. Four years ago, Ms. Mayse learned that the Moores, a longtime family on the block, were retiring and moving. Sick of apartments and looking for tax breaks, she bought the Moore house for $27,500. In the middle of negotiations, she listened incredulously as a black Realtor asked her: "Why do you want to live over here if you have a law degree?"

Sitting in her living room, Ms. Mayse shakes her head. "It drives me crazy. People don't want to make things work. I know that there are some cops who would rather be in North Dallas giving cute white girls tickets. They don't want to be here," she says. "I know that."

Last year, she attended the funeral of Fred and Mildred Finch, the prominent civil rights activists, who were murdered in their South Dallas home. Standing at the funeral, Ms. Mayse wept like a child. Even with all the tragedy in her own family, she had never felt like leaving South Dallas. It would be, she thought, an act of abandonment. Now, though, she dwelled on leaving the neighborhood she had returned to. "I can't find any peace," she told friends.

Marilynn Mayse settled down. She thought more and more about the police in her neighborhood. She thought she understood how their frustrations might actually be similar to her own. "Now, to me, when the police shoot somebody who seems to deserve it, it doesn't bother me at all," she tells me.

It is quiet outside. The only sound is the rhythmic thud of a basketball hitting the ground. "When they kill them, I don't care. Hey, I'd come out with my guns. I could never be a policeman. I'd be tried for murder right away."

Hudson Griffin, the unofficial mayor of the black community, passed away in 1991. His memorial service was considered so important it was carried, live, on a local radio station. There is no real qualitative way to gauge ease and unease, especially as it relates to public perception of the police. Perception, reality, and race still define the relationship. The new police headquarters for the city was built in South Dallas in 2003. The Dallas Citizens Police Review Board continues to hear complaints.

PART THREE
THE MUSIC

PHOTOCHEMICAL BLUES

My wife and I had dropped in on Alex Moore at his home, not far from Oak-land Avenue. We just knocked on the door and he said to come in. He seemed to laugh all the time. I sat in his parlor, and he played and played on a console piano with a big urn of plastic pink and white tulips on it. His piano was also decorated with a small white figurine of a horse with its right front leg raised. He gave me one of his cards and told me to stay in touch. And he was, in his way, a gateway to the musical history of Texas. He embodied several traditions that could be traced back to the influential Deep Ellum area, and he was the last of a kind. Moore's life and music, like those of Robert Shaw and other Texas piano players who still performed in the 1980s, could explain the growth of the state, the way the place had been built, upon whose backs it had been built. He had been born in Freedman's Town. He had gone to Colored School Number 2. His music was about Texas, about staying mobile in the face of fate and circumstance. He was one of the messengers, the advance scouts, for so many things that Langston Hughes wrote about.

When I went to his memorial service, an earnest white man stood up and seemed to take a lot of credit for Moore's life and times. I might have misinterpreted it. But I was sure that wherever he was, Moore was laughing his ass off.

Through four or five desk changes over several years, the photo of the old bluesman traveled with me. Up it goes over each new desk. It finally flips into the supremely totemic stage: a photochemical talisman. Take it down and you die.

The picture shows a gray-bearded old-timer sitting in a tiny wood-paneled room. His dark fingers are like long, weathered sticks blown off a tree.

Alex Moore, 1984. Photo by Randy Eli Grothe.

His hands, one of them with a rubber band wrapped around the wrist, are pieces of bark draped over his lap. The plastic clock on the wall is frozen at 7:02. A plastic horse stands atop a cheap upright piano. Plastic flowers rest next to the plastic horse. And the old man's head is thrown back over his left shoulder. People who look hard at the picture don't know that Alex Moore is enjoying a deep belly laugh. Eyes closed and mouth open, he could almost be registering a sharp pain in his chest.

When I take my wife to meet him, minutes before the photo is taken, he tells us to sit on a tattered green couch. He plays the piano for us; rollicking tunes about secret delights in the old quarters of Deep Ellum. When I shake Moore's hand, he folds his two hands on top of one of mine. He will not let go until my face flushes with surprise. As I leave his little house in South Dallas, Moore asks whether he is going to get paid for the interview. Fifteen dollars would be nice. I tell him no. He laughs over and over again.

Moore stands at his wooden, peeling doorway. He smiles from behind the screen and watches us pull away on the unpaved patch of dirt. The next few years, deep into his eighties, Moore plays piano at the occasional festival. He is given awards. And very little cash. Moore spends hours playing dominoes at the Martin Luther King Center. People interview him about his days playing music in Deep Ellum. Earnest musicologists trail him with cameras.

Still no money. And exactly a year ago, Moore sat down and carefully wrote a letter to Alto McGowan. His old friend, and funeral home operator, knew what it was about even before he sliced it open.

"He wanted me to bury him sometime. I guess he was getting things together," McGowan tells me.

One Friday night, Moore slowly walked to the Packing House Market. He bought two bags of food and lugged the heavy sacks back to the bus stop. Alex Moore was eighty-nine, and people that age should never have to wait at bus stops. People that age should never stand alone at night, big brown bags of groceries tucked under their arms.

A few minutes later, his meats and vegetables went skidding across the floor of a Dallas Area Rapid Transit bus. Moore probably has a look on his face like the one in my photograph. Like mine when he wouldn't let go of my hand.

The funeral arrangements take a few days to figure out. There is no cash. Friends, including McGowan, help. And Moore's son, a postal worker, wonders why his father didn't call him that night for a ride home. "He lived his life the way he wanted to. He believed in himself. He said that was his trademark. Believing in himself made him different from everybody else," his son tells me.

The last bluesman's funeral I went to was in Houston six or seven years ago. Lightnin' Hopkins had surrendered to a few decades of unsuccessfully running out from under the shadows that invested his music with the raw, sad taste of real life. The line snaked around the block. We waited in the chill evening for our turns to trod across the rickety floorboards. Hopkins was laid out nice and pretty. He looked like he was floating on a sea of prom corsages and pastel-colored taffy. Hopkins, with skeptical eyes, would have appreciated the irony. Reporters from big magazines were there. So was a chunky millionaire from ZZ Top. Still, no cash. Alex Moore could relate. "My father had no money," says Moore's son. "He never made the money that he should have. But I'll tell you what: My father was a happy, happy man. He was very unusual."

I have a blue business card in a keepsake drawer. It is in there with an old knife that belonged to my father and a faded Western Union telegram I sent to a woman I knew, proposing marriage. There is also a piece of coral that belonged to my ancient relatives: some Italians believe tiny pieces of coral are talismans, ways to ward off evil. Next to all of this is that blue card that Alex Moore gave me. It has his name on it, and in big letters it reads: "PIANOIST." He died in 1989. On November 22, 1988, the State of Texas had declared his birthday "Alex Moore Day." In 1987, he had become the first African American Texan to receive a National Heritage Fellowship from the National Endowment for the Arts.

SEARCHIN' BLUES

I had read Helen Dance's excellent biography of T-Bone Walker, and it was filled with secrets about Dallas, about the Oak Cliff zone. T-Bone had, to me, changed everything. There should have been a T-Bone Texas Toll Road decades ago. I followed the signs in her book and began to see whether there were any direct vestiges of Walker's life in Dallas. That was the hard part. The easy part was finding pieces of his musical legacy. He had put an elegant cape on the rural blues that he learned from Blind Lemon Jefferson. He had gone uptown, immaculate in his demeanor and presentation. And Dallas, if anything, had inherited that, channeled that. If there was still a black blues tradition in Dallas, it was mostly defined by what Z. Z. Hill, Johnnie Taylor, and all of their musical descendants had left behind. An uptown sound, a soulful sound, something more urban and less country. It was something you could trace all the way back to T-Bone Walker—he took the guitar to the city and then some. He took it around the world, made it palatable, made it essential. And he played the guitar the way people learned to survive. To get over. With patience, even elegance, in the face of uncertainties and abject cruelties. Some of his records almost seem understated in an age of excess. And that might be the point today. T-Bone Walker exuded grace. And it was staggering to wander Dallas and Fort Worth, going to club after club after club, and hearing people invoke not just his sound . . . but his name.

Reportorial distance is a funny, elusive thing. Some writers in New York, in the early 1960s, openly talked about their "struggle for subjectivity." About trying to "allow" their biases and beliefs into their work. Most mainstream journalists still resist the notion. It was, is, hard when it comes to the blues. It is almost an oxymoron, the notion of objectively approaching the blues. I spent weeks work-

ing on this story, staying out late, trying to filter what I was seeing through what I was feeling. The entire history of a state sometimes seemed to play out in a song in a club at the dark end of a street. There were those moments of painful clarity when the hum of music, sex, broken promises, lies, and laughter would all collide—and then it was back to the starting point, back to trying to understand the blues of Langston Hughes. It was the same, really, and all the clubs that I visited for this story could be any one of a thousand clubs over time—the ones where Big Joe Turner played, where Jimmy Reed played, where Funny Papa Smith played.

Patty Jack Lott, late of Oak Cliff, Texas, is on the line from Los Angeles, trying to tell me where to begin looking. Lott abandoned the state decades ago, following the migratory pattern of so many Texas African Americans to California, but he knows how and where the sound bubbled out of Dallas's gumbo soil. He is talking about blues music—about what he sees as Dallas's gift to the world—and about standing on The Bottom, watching the river rise with his good friend, the musician Thibeaux.

"That's where he learned the blues, and if you don't go down to The Bottom yourself, you won't know what the hell I'm talking about," growls Patty Jack, who has become an unofficial musicologist on all things Texas. In his seventies, he has earned the right to light a short fuse: "It began on The Bottom. We had the church, the river, and the music."

Geographically, The Bottom is really The Bottoms, where nature, racism, and religion conspired to help breed the blues along the south banks of the Trinity River, directly opposite downtown Dallas. Where a community survived floods that rose like painful and predictable sorrows. Survived outbreaks of tuberculosis in the 1940s. Survived the splintering effects of Interstate 35 in the 1950s. It is also where Thibeaux—guitarist, composer, and vocalist Aaron "T-Bone" Walker—spent his formative years in the 1920s, messing around with his best friend, Patty Jack Lott.

If you study the anemic doctoral dissertations, the mercurial Walker is often credited with being the man who delivered, through his blues-based vocabulary, the electric guitar to the world. On the quick list of things Texas has done to put the earth's axis on a new angle, that fact may outstrip them all. Like it or not, the electric guitar was the instrument of social revolution. The thing that made kids leave home. Made sex more popular. Drugs, too. It gave careers to a whole new league of preachers, oily underassistant West Coast promotion men, and *Time* magazine essayists. And the fact that a case can be made for tracing it back to someone who stood in The Bottoms of Oak Cliff is enough to make you wonder where the statues are. Musicologist

Pete Welding's words can go on the base: "He participated in and contributed to virtually every development black vernacular music has witnessed in the last half-century. A number of them he initiated as well."

But there is no statue. Instead, Texas makes do with Walker's legacy, the movable feast of clubs where the vagaries of people's own personal floods, marauding highways, or wracking bodily pains are still—ironically—celebrated. The Bottoms remain alive. Ignore the skyline of downtown Dallas, looming to the north, and things look as they did fifty years ago. And the anthems to Dallas's unsteady times that came out of The Bottoms are also still alive. But time and tolerance have spread the musical legacy of The Bottoms to other public and personal outposts.

Misery really doesn't discriminate.

And Walker's first record, cut a few weeks before Christmas 1929 under the name "Oak Cliff T-Bone," is the still appropriate "Trinity River Blues." Accompanied by Dallasite Doug Finnel on piano, Walker sings:

> Trinity River Blues keep me bothered all the time.
> I lose all my clothes, baby, believe I'm going to lose my mind . . .
> Trinity River rising, it came in my windows and doors.

Duke Robillard, a popular white musician, has given a lot of thought to the fact that the actual act of performing music, the kinetic presentation, seems no longer enough for most audiences. People need a message, a calling, a big answer or question—or the event and sound are not as valuable. A few decades ago, the simple act of performing the music was the message. One Saturday night, Robillard's theory is being tested at Booker's Arandas Club, once the home of jazz legend Red Garland, at the intersection of Oakland Avenue and Hatcher Street.

According to James "Foots" Snipes, the maintenance man who has kept the Arandas working for thirty years, the place has "livened up a bit" since it went to a blues format. The Arandas has an honorable history; once known as the Captain's Table and then the Metropole, the club was home to the best informal jazz. Garland came home here, back to Dallas, after he had done what he needed and wanted to do, playing for kings and queens—and with Miles Davis, John Coltrane, and everyone else. Garland came home, in his way, to a place where nothing had changed. He came home, maybe in search of the blues, and found that the bedrock was still there: the music and all the things that fed the music, willed the music into reality, that defined the music. Every aching, bittersweet blues building block was . . . still there in

Texas. Red Garland was a god in Europe, Japan, and New York City . . . and he came back to spend his last years playing, mostly unattended, in a dark club in a part of town that hadn't really changed since he grew up.

After I pay Gwen two dollars at the door, a young woman in a lusty red dress acts as a guide for me and two friends through the low-ceilinged, packed nightclub. From the outside, the Arandas looks like an airplane hangar for dwarves. Inside, it unfolds and stretches forward. Dark red lights, the rustling of skirts, spicy colognes, and waitresses whisking by with platters. People are chasing me with their eyes. In the middle of a thumping song, James Braggs—his blues band has been a regular at Arandas for years—turns and trails the three newcomers as they wind their way to a corner table. He is grinning and oozing the lyrics to a Clarence Carter tune: "What time do YOU like to make love? Do you like to make love before breakfast?"

A lot of people in the Arandas know what time they like to make love. They tell Braggs. We quietly slide into chairs pressed against each other. "I hope you two are lovers," the waitress whispers in my ear and nodding at the woman next to me.

Five minutes later, a giant-sized woman is shadowing the table, insisting that someone dance with her. James Braggs has ordered his band into a hypnotic rendition of the late Z. Z. Hill's instant classic, "Down Home Blues." The song, a huge seller, marked a pivotal moment in recording history because it is credited with bringing blues back to black audiences in the 1980s and 1990s. For years it was an anthem, a song heard at "Blue Monday" nightclub parties, those special after-work soirees meant to beat back the dawn of another grinding workweek. For years it was the required, demanded, song at clubs all across Texas—The Web Lounge in San Antonio, The Branding Stable or Club Laveek or Garcia's in Houston, all the little clubs that change names every few years in Elgin, Tyler, and Mexia.

Braggs has a habit of measuring his room and adjusting the length of each song. His brother is the famous songwriter and bandleader Al "TNT" Braggs. He knows what he is doing, and he knows what Time It Is. The glowing neon clocks have ticked past midnight. People are sated from devouring the big plates of chicken and dumplings that owner Booker McGill has laid out, gratis, for his lovers and dancers. Braggs knows they are in a slow, easy mood. He downshifts into a slithering, endless version of the Z. Z. Hill sermon. He gets rhetorical: "Do you mind if I get comfortable?" A fine mist of sweat dampens my forehead. My new special friend is dipping her body, rolling her eyes into her skull, and taking up a lot of space on the dance floor.

The dance area, tiny enough to begin with, is brimming over. The thirty dancers are brushing up against a far wall, touching the small stage, bumping into tables, and becoming one pulsating amoeba. Without warning, a thin light comes on over my head, as if someone is throwing a beaming practical joke on me. Just as quickly, a hand rises from the middle of the crowd and slowly unscrews the naked lightbulb. The room is darker, the ceiling seems lower, and the laughter louder. Z. Z. Hill's song goes like this: "Give me some of those down home blues."

James Braggs is sitting in the back of his comfortable house down the block from Roosevelt High School, close to where Eighth Street abruptly becomes Bonnie View Road. Braggs has played with the best blues musicians in America—B. B. King, T-Bone Walker, Freddie King, and Bobby "Blue" Bland. When he was a kid, he walked up and down Spring Avenue in the shadow of Fair Park, singing old Jimmy Reed songs. Braggs would duck out of his apartment in the projects and stare in the window of a little club called The Gold Mine. When he got older, he learned the guitar from local legend Cal Valentine. When he was a teenager, he played with his hero Jimmy Reed. "When you go to other cities, people know about Dallas. They know about the history, the influential musicians. The reputation is around the country, really, around the world. It has gotten to the point where blues musicians are moving to Dallas from other parts of the country. Little Joe Blue, Vernon Garrett, Barbara Morrison—they've all come to Dallas to work.

"You can go out any night of the week and hear blues in Dallas. Dozens of places have it. But I really think there is a difference between what you get. To me, if you want to hear the blues, to experience it the way it was meant by the people who invented it, then you better come to South Dallas."

All right then. Hop Wilson said it best. He was the Houston man famous for what he called "ghetto blues." You had to go into the alley, he said. You had to go into the night and whatever was beyond the night. There were all these places you had to go, so many places in Texas, over so many years. You had to go to Egypt, Texas, and listen to the blues band playing at the all-black rodeo, the one put on by the Southern Negro Cowboy Association. You had to go to Brother's Record Store in Abilene, hidden and hanging on. You had to listen to the music gurgling up behind the counter at Turnerhill's Barbecue in Abilene. And in Carter's Barbecue in Dallas, and in Adam's Rib, the barbecue shack up the hill from the old Dallas zoo. And, yeah, you had to go to the Third, Fourth, and Fifth Wards. You had to stand out on Lyons Avenue, the most intense stretch of street in the state of Texas, and listen to the blues ghosts moaning up and down the zone they called Pearl Harbor, all up and down the sidewalk in front of the legendary Stanley's House of Power. You can buy things in Stanley's. When faith was all you had—a condition that applied to nearly everyone along this stretch of Lyons—then you had to go into Stanley's and buy graveyard dust, John the Conqueror roots, coffin nails, and anything else that could "get you over." That was how Hop Wilson put it: "I done got over at last." You spend your day, your week, your damned life trying to "get over," to stave off whatever needs staving off. The people around you. Those ghosts. The police. The walls. The history. The misery. All of it. You pray, you play, you gamble that you can "get over." And maybe, as Hop Wilson sang, "I done got over and I can face the people with a smile." You go to South Dallas, deep along East Commerce Street in San Antonio, you walk down Elysian Street in Houston, you slip along the side streets in Pittsburg, and you know the ghosts are damned sure there . . . you know what everyone else knows, as if it happened yesterday . . . when the mob came in 1941, just before we entered World War II, and castrated that black man who had the bad luck to be visiting from Dallas. And you wonder what else you don't know, what else is out there, what else is being held over your head like some immutable force of history. It is you, of course. You are the history, come to visit like something on horseback, long ago, outside the window and thudding down the muddy lane, coming out of the trees . . . the worst kind of visitor, the unwanted visitor. No good will come of your being here. No one invited you. And off you go to South Dallas in search of the blues, as if they were yours . . . as if you didn't help give people the blues.

On my way out of Booker's Arandas, Booker McGill asks me: "Are we doing anything wrong?" Booker thinks he has been visited by the police. So, it turns out, did half the people in the place. A few years earlier, the legendary Jasper Baccus, a big man who ran the nearby and justly famous Baccus Cleaners for years on Martin Luther King, Jr. Boulevard, chased me out of his store. I had come to find out what people were thinking on the street, in South Dallas, and Baccus wasn't having any of it. He ran out from behind his counter, ran into the street, flapping his arms and screaming: "You're not a reporter, I don't know what you want, but you better leave." That is sometimes the way it goes in South Dallas. The scary characters who walked in the shadows—like Albino George and Chicago Red—thought that any white people in South Dallas were probably undercover cops. So did Emerson Emory, maybe the last doctor to make house calls in a big city in Texas. So did Hudson Griffin, who presided over all kinds of problems from his lair at his Oakland Avenue tailor's shop. So did the guy behind the counter at Black Jack Pizza. And the bartender who ran the after-hours back room at The Green Parrot Lounge, where I would watch musicians, gamblers, and off-duty cops knock back tumblers of something dark until the sun came rising up over the Trinity River. At Club Arandas, James Braggs thought for a split second that I was a talent scout. He was an optimist.

Later that morning, at the 3100 Club on Grand Avenue, the soul singers Vernon Garrett and Barbara Morrison are being backed by the Moore Brothers, who cruise Dallas in a white van that says "Live R&B" on the side. And Earnest Davis, the peripatetic former owner of a short-lived blues institution called The Classic Club, is holding forth at a prime table. Starting in 1982, Davis, who travels with a big rhinestone *E* on his lapel, became one of the first entrepreneurs to go back to the future with the blues. The best in Dallas came to his club, advertised as "Where Smart People Meet": Z. Z. Hill, Charlie Roberson, Vernon Garrett, Gregg Smith, R. L. "The Right Reverend of the Blues" Griffin, Little Joe Blue, Smokin' Joe, and Lucky Peterson. And in a throwback to the time when blues shows were occasionally interrupted by some talented tap dancers, Davis would halt a blues set and invite teenagers in sunglasses and hooded sweatshirts—kids who, on looks alone, had caused half the members of the audience to lean toward the exits—to push back tables and break-dance on the floor. He pushed the envelope: On some nights he went to the stage to introduce "Mr. Aretha Franklin," a sturdy-looking black man who happened to be wearing a long dress. No makeup, no other feminine affectation. Just a long dress. The singer looked like a middle linebacker, maybe a power forward in basketball, and he sounded just like Aretha Franklin. Wags in the audience, brave in the dark, would yell out: "Sing 'you make me feel like a natural woman'!" Earnest Davis knew that the blues people, the night people, had to be served, and that half of them wouldn't blink an eye at a man in drag singing Aretha songs. It was, a lot of customers said, a nod to the days when stuff like that was copasetic down in Deep Ellum, or on Bourbon Street, or, hell, in Harlem.

Even with the food devoured—the 3100 has a Saturday-night fish fry—and it being close to two, the club still has a nice crowd. Clarence Turner, the owner, is watching me as he leans against a wall. Turner has printed up shimmering gold business cards that say the 3100 Club is "The Social Club To Be." And suddenly, Earnest Davis insists I follow him to Meadow Street. There, the soul-blues singer R. L. Griffin is trying to unearth an old tradition, the after-hours blues club. At one time, Dallas was famous for its pre-church, early-morning venues: places where whole generations grew up in a hurry, where the best musicians would play for free, where people would leave at sunrise and go straight to church.

Earnest is like a mad but good tour guide. He trusts me—after I pass a little test. Late one night he shows me his key chain and asks me to identify what kind of car he drives. I correctly answer "Mercedes Benz," and he calls for a drink to be delivered to our table. He leans in and he tells me stories. Mad stories that swirl in the night and spin round and round until I realize that Earnest is watching me closely, watching to see what I do when he says that he once had some trouble with a woman he knew real well and he had to take out his golf clubs and, well, he had to smack out her car headlights. And to show that I find it all perfectly reasonable, I ask him whether he used his woods. And he studies me for what seems like a full minute and then yells out, his voice rising above the bubbling blues guitar and that special sound of silk dresses rubbing up against silk suits: "Hell no, I wouldn't waste my woods that way. C'mon man, I used my irons."

I stop the microfilm machine at the May 23, 1942, edition of the *Dallas Express*. Filled with photographs and first-person stories, the defunct newspaper for the black community is a primary source for understanding Dallas's blues ranking. That week in the middle of World War II, the paper read: "Doris Standifer, the blues shouter on the main stem, is rounding out her fifth year as a box office attraction in Dallas . . . Born with the gift, her contralto singing is one reason why the crowds have followed her to every nitery where she has appeared . . . Her interpretation, feeling and warmth all have made her Dallas' delineator songstress of note . . . Terrific Doris Standifer . . . the No. 1 Lady of Song in Texas."

I make a few phone calls. And later, Doris Standifer, her voice like some blues chef's concoction of Grand Marnier, peach syrup, and the menthol tang of a Kool cigarette, is asking me: "Are you sure you want to talk to me?"

Why, yes. Yes, I do.

Standifer lives not far from where James Braggs spent his formative years wandering up and down Spring Avenue and pretending he was the great bluesman Jimmy Reed. Her house is down the block from two neighborhood institutions, Urso's grocery store and the original Carter's barbecue palace, where the Carter family produces sweet-potato pies blessed by their investment in Freestone County yams. In her dark living room, on top of the tiny television, is a framed photograph of a stunning young woman, her face tilted up and one shoulder bared. At the time Standifer had the picture taken, she would open carefully sealed envelopes with adoring letters inside that began: "Dear Queen Of The Blues . . ."

She sits in her chair, dressed as if she were going on the SS *United States* ("fastest ship in the world") on a 1950s trip to Marseille. Some people take care of themselves when they walk out the door. Some people care about what they look like all the time. Doris Standifer never really stopped being the Queen of the Blues. "I was fifteen and I was slipping," she tells me. "I just loved the blues. I tried to have it both ways." At first she tried to stay clear of the music, the clubs, the sharp-dressed people, and the clinking glasses. The names made her dizzy: Nat Towles's Harlem Niteclub, Lucky Millinder's Rockin' In Rhythm Show, Dorothy Mayes's Open Door, the Rose Ballroom.

Her mother, a gospel singer in the sanctified church, warned her it was the devil's music. One day in the 1930s, a next-door neighbor heard the teenager singing in the backyard on Lucille Street. The neighbor told her a club was looking for an entertainer, and the teenager left her house late on a Saturday night. When she returned, at five in the morning, her mother was up waiting for her. She seemed resigned. "Say your prayers before you hit the floor of this house," her mother demanded. "And no point in going to bed. Change your clothes because we're going to church."

Standifer looks at her old photograph. She really hasn't changed much. "I'm just thankful I didn't fall into the wrong hands," she tells me.

She came close, staying up late and accepting tumblers of gold-colored liquid from suave gangsters. "I turned grown-up when I was singing. The blues players, especially T-Bone, sent for me. I went to Los Angeles, Kansas City, Memphis," she says. "Then my parents got sick and they needed me. I just let it all go and became a maid. Even after I quit, I had so many people looking down on me for singing the blues. Well, if I want to sing the blues, I will. This is my life. God gave it to me. I don't owe any explanations to anyone else. They don't wake me up, and they don't put me to sleep at night."

For years, forever, I can see her in my mind only as the woman in that picture on top of her TV. She never went back to music, at least not to the kind of music that made her the Queen of the Blues. A friend of mine tried to coax her back into the life, into performing again, into recording some songs. I think she preferred to keep all of it tucked away. And she seemed, that day I went to see her, as if she were expecting me. As if time had stood still, or as if she had seen so many things in her life, enough to satisfy her, that nothing could ever surprise her again.

Wellington's, on Second Avenue, just south of Hatcher Street, was once the most stylish blues club in North Texas. Suits and ties and the slick Los Angeles–bred blues of Vernon Garrett and Little Joe Blue. Wellington's had a Blue Monday special: nothing but blues was performed on the first day of a fresh working week, a fresh week of starting all over on the killing floor. And there was Sadler's Corner (which occasionally featured Little James Everett, Z. Z. Hill's cousin), Tricia's, Sonny's Cocktail Lounge, and the Cowboy Lounge. And, of course, there was The Bluebird, in Fort Worth, south of Interstate 30 on Horne.

Alex Moore, Dallas's venerable blues pianist, would recognize The Bluebird as the direct descendant of the "chockhouses," the bootleg-liquor joints that operated during Prohibition. Not many clubs could be like it in America: maybe Booba Barnes's Playboy Nightclub on Nelson Street in Greenville, Mississippi, came close. So did Garcia Milburn's club in Houston's Heights area, where a man named Winchester sang old Mance Lipscomb blues songs.

The Bluebird was always in a permanent state of decay, tilting toward the street. The bend in the building made the booths look like a line of old-time roller-coaster cars fading into a curve. The Jiffy Pop popcorn was made on what looks like a turntable, and it was brought to your table by a midget who turned surly if you didn't let him dance with your date. The Bluebird was also the most integrated—racially and economically—club in Texas. On the dance floor, a 300-plus-pound man in overalls was rubbing a paw over his stubbly beard and breathing heavily through his mouth. He was gyrating with a blonde woman in a black leather miniskirt and an expensive-looking white sweater. A reed-thin man with a baseball cap was banging a stick on an empty beer can. Two burly guys in leather coats and cowboy hats were guffawing with two tiny women with beehive hair. Three yuppies were in a booth staring down at the piles of meat they had brought in from Red's Como Barbecue across the street. Alongside them, the four-foot-high waiter was smiling down at the ribs and clapping his hands as if he were in a Holy Ghost church on Sunday morning.

One Saturday night, the immortal Robert Ealey had just settled into a cracked plastic chair, and I saw him carefully unwrap another plastic-tipped Swisher Sweet. His head enveloped in smoke, he was about to sip on a sweating can of Coors. He looked up as a froggy voice echoed: "Ladies and gentlemen, we are lucky to have in the house tonight the fabulous Robert Ealey. Give him a big hand."

Ealey glided to the small cluttered bandstand and tossed out three straight tunes by Joe Tex, Memphis Slim, and the Staple Singers. He changed the words of the songs, made jokes, sipped more beer, waved his hand, and left: he and guitar player U. P. Wilson, who does a crowd-pleasing imitation, on guitar, of a one-handed cellist who likes to smoke unfiltered cigarettes, had a date at Jim's Food and Blues on Camp Bowie Boulevard. There, a retro hipster in a 1940s, all-electric red suit and red patent leather shoes manned the door, and waitresses pushed two-dollar plastic glasses of schnapps. But Ealey would be back at The Bluebird before the sun rises.

As Ealey disappeared into the dirt parking lot and the haze of smoke coming from Red's, the trumpet player in the house band was rambling on in a voice that sounded like Yogi Bear standing at the bottom of a well: "Yes, yes, yes . . . love, peace, and happiness . . . If you got money, that's just gravy . . . You hear a lot of jokes about money lately . . . and they're still not funny . . . Hello, ladies and gentlemen . . . welcome to the west side of Fort Worth, where the women are good looking, the men are strong, and the children are just a little bit above average."

Two nights ago, Zuzu Bollin had bounded to the stage and stared out at a sea of white faces in Club Dada, in Deep Ellum. He was trying to make a comeback. Now, this rainy afternoon, he is holed up in one of the few remaining houses in the State-Thomas neighborhood, the old area once known as North Dallas, before gentrification and highways and arson and a bundle of political tricks caused that vital black zone to be turned into a maze of office buildings and empty lots where condos will be built.

"Welcome," he says to me. "Bet you're wondering what happened to North Dallas. Well, they took it away."

From Bollin's one-room apartment, he can see the empty fields that once were filled with the meat and soul of black Dallas. The churches, schools, restaurants, and nightclubs were all torn down. And people who lived there remember looking out their windows at night as white men with gas cans scrambled away from another church that they had set on fire. Set fire to the churches and the niggers will scatter—it was, some said, as easy as that. Once they were gone from their squalid shotgun shacks, the now-valuable downtown real estate was easy to scoop up and sell to developers, to high rollers, to city planners. Who cares whether famous black Americans like Hall of Famer Ernie Banks came from old North Dallas? Who really cares? Neighborhoods were malleable—well, some neighborhoods were.

"Things were jumping around the corner here," says Zuzu, a singer and guitar player who was a star in the 1950s. "I came to Dallas in 1950. My head was filled with musicians." Texas musical gods, the men who drifted the highways and slept in the homes of their fans and never seemed to pay for a meal or a drink—and who always had to be paid in cash after their gigs. Little Son Jackson, Doctor Clayton, Leroy Carr, Blind Lemon Jefferson, T-Bone Walker, Mercy Baby, and Frankie Lee Simms: they were all connected, one way or another, and they all made the rounds in Texas. Most of them knew, or knew about, one another. It was a Texas thing, and you wouldn't understand . . . unless you were from Texas, unless you knew the way Texas operated, unless you survived Texas like you were all communists and you had to call each other fellow travelers. You had to know the blues in order to get the blues, in order to know how deep the blues musicians were, how brave they were, how they were the itinerant oral historians, the black equivalent of the Mexican men who wandered South Texas and San Antonio, singing their *corridos*, the songs that relayed the news, the times, the temperament. Zuzu Bollin knew it. It was as if it had been born inside of him. "I grew up with all kinds of people saying to stay away from the blues. But it was something you couldn't stay away from."

Bollin grew up in Frisco, Texas. At night he heard sounds snaking across the floorboards. The bootleg-liquor house was next door. Bollin tossed and turned, listening to the squeals of laughter, the hushed silence as the dice hit the ground, the scraping sounds of dancing feet moving back and forth. "It was more than I could stand."

In 1950, he moved to Dallas, and everything was locked up tight by the cops and gangsters and preachers; everyone knew it. When Zuzu Bollin hit the city, everyone told him he was going to be a national star. People couldn't get enough of his records: Bollin's voice and guitar seemed to jump off the discs. He had a rumbling sound, the deepest, most rounded voice imaginable. It wasn't a primordial sound like Howlin' Wolf's; it was a giant orb of a sound, like a tenor sax at its most encompassing level. His voice was like a big boulder, the kind that comes over a ridge, at night, thick and thudding and insistent. People were knocked out by it—and thrilled by it. Women assumed he was a lover. Men assumed he was a fighter.

Then, Jack Ruby developed a problem with him over Bollin's pay after he played at one of Ruby's downtown clubs. Ruby drummed out his own little blues song for Bollin: all of Bollin's records were pulled off the air by local radio stations. The chance for a breakaway hit, the thing that would have lifted him from Dallas, was squashed.

Doris Standifer, the Queen of the Blues, became a maid. Zuzu Bollin, the man with the sixteen-ton blues voice, went to work pressing pants for a living. And for decades, he just understood it to be that way. That was the way it was. It wasn't just him. There were a hundred more. And, obviously, not just blues musicians. You stayed out of certain parts of town, you kept your head down, you found solace in stolen moments.

Chuck Nevitt, the most sympathetic blues archivist in Texas, found Bollin in an Allen Street boardinghouse. Now, the two of them stay up late talking about the music, Nevitt urging Bollin to practice on an old acoustic guitar. They sometimes stop and talk about whether things have changed since Aaron "Thibeaux" Walker left the Trinity River bottoms. When Bollin arrived in Dallas, he lived in West Dallas, near the Trinity River. There was a boat tied to a stick on the riverbank. He and other people in the neighborhood would use it to row down to a spot closer to where the city buses would stop.

"Do you know that old T-Bone Walker song about the Trinity River?" Bollin asks me, his face framed by a mushroom cloud of cigarette smoke. The skin looks shiny on his face, as if it has been seared or stretched onto the bone. Some people say that when you hit the crack pipe, your skin starts looking like thin, wet clothing stuck to your body, clinging to your infrastructure for dear life.

"When that river rose," he tells me, "you had to take care of yourself."

Many of the players and clubs have gone away: Zuzu Bollin died in 1990. Booker's Arandas closed in 2006, ending a deep chapter in Texas music. Robert Ealey died in 2001. One very astute writer in Fort Worth said, "Robert died of lingering complications—as much a matter of demoralization, I believe, as physical injury." He died, in other words, from the blues. The Bluebird closed and opened again. Texas still has one of the richest roots blues scenes in the world, particularly in Dallas and Houston and small towns throughout East Texas, where some things, for better or worse, never really change.

Henry Qualls, 1994. Photo by Scotty Ferris.

LAST MAN BLUES

My friend Chuck Nevitt called me one day and said he had heard about a musician out in the countryside, in a place called Elmo, Texas. Nevitt is a selfless man, consumed by some bottomless passion for the blues and social justice. I had seen him personally resurrect Zuzu Bollin, trying to get him recognized again, recorded again, and trying to fend off all the demons, including crack, that were chasing the old blues artist. I knew Chuck was a good man when I heard he used to drive the fragile Zuzu to a hidden spot in Oak Cliff where a woman made the best sno-cones in the city. One time I had a house party, and Chuck brought the singer and harp player Sam Myers, a towering genius who had brought his Mississippi blues to Texas. And Chuck and I had talked one time about the idea of his resurrecting Peppermint Harris in Houston. He tried to find him, but I think Peppermint had already slipped away. So when he called and said that I should come with him to see Henry Qualls, I didn't hesitate. I could hear the excitement in his voice. He said it was like going back in time. And despite the fact that some parts of the Texas past should never be revisited, I went with him.

I visited Henry Qualls several times, and I was almost suspicious at first. It was as if central casting had crafted a bit of mythology. But I knew he was the real thing when he talked about the rich housewives in Highland Park, the rich enclave inside Dallas. He said they had nothing to do during the day but lie by the pool and watch the black man cut the lawn. He gave me some muscadine wine, which I had never had. He talked about roots, potions. I took a friend to see Qualls one night. My friend played guitar, and he sat in at the jam at Qualls's crumbling house. There was some sort of roaring heater filled with flame. Outside, a big rusted pipe, probably scavenged from an old East Texas oil rig, was

being used for a barbecue pit. It was raining like the end of the world. When we
finally left, we ran through the downpour toward a little roadside diner in East
Texas. We were out of breath, soaked, and the families inside turned to stare at us.
We were strangers, and we smelled, I suspected, of whiskey, smoke, and charred
meat. The waitress was wary, stiff, formal. The diner grew hushed. My friend, a
wag, said sotto voce: "Damn, it's good to finally be out of prison."

I went back to see Qualls, and I saw him in Dallas also. He was always more
comfortable at his country home. I knew, as I was writing down the things he said,
that he was smiling. And I suspected he knew that I was his willing servant.

A Texas music promoter felt sure that he had come across one of the most
important discoveries in recent Texas history. Now, alone in his two-
room garage apartment, he placed a call to Holland. Waiting on the other
end was the producer of a prestigious European music festival.

The Texas promoter pushed the Start button on his tape player and placed
his phone near the speakers. Over the wires moved a slow, naked sound from
somewhere long ago. Spider-web whispers of a rough backwoods East Texas
guitar rhythm rarely heard in the last quarter century. Open-wound sighs
of an instrument—bottle, knife, shard of glass?—hitting steel strings. And
most of all, a proud but weary workingman's voice. A broken, graveyard
voice singing . . . about the train, the phantom, that might take you away if
only someone would let you on board . . . about a thing so cold it could only
be death . . . about the cruel way a child, of any age, can lose a mother.

The Dutch producer listened to the haunted echoes from a forgotten corner of Texas. It was, he thought, stranded in time. It was a musical history
of early black life in Deep East Texas, a documentary of the smothering poverty, the aching racism, the quiet triumphs, and the stolen pleasures. It was
an unpolished sound he thought had been exiled to scratchy records and
the aping efforts of earnest white imitators. It was a singular school of country music that traced a straight line to the very Texans who had invented
the blues and, ultimately, rock 'n' roll. The European producer listened to a
doomed man's defiant plea: "I shall not be moved . . . on my way to heaven
. . . Just like a train . . . I shall not be moved . . . on my way to heaven . . . I
shall not be moved."

The Texas promoter felt sure that the old man on the tape was the real
thing. "How should I put this? When you realize that it has been more
than thirty years since anybody has come on the scene who plays this kind
of music, it didn't take Einstein to figure out this was important," he told
people. To make sure, he sent a copy of his tape to a well-known musicolo-

gist from Mississippi who had worked for decades with American legends Son House, Lightnin' Hopkins, Mance Lipscomb, and Fred McDowell. The man from Mississippi said he heard distinct shades of Blind Willie Johnson in that music from East Texas. And for his money, he added, Blind Willie Johnson, who recorded in the 1920s, was the greatest gospel singer who had ever lived.

Now, as the tape being played over those international phone lines finally clicked to a halt, the Texas promoter braced for the reaction from overseas. The first thing the Dutch producer uttered was "hired." Sight unseen, the sixty-something-year-old man on the tape became the first person booked for the producer's annual international music gathering. The hard-drinking man on the tape—Henry Qualls from Elmo, Texas—was about to embark on the biggest trip of his life. A trip that would take him to photo sessions with men who provide photographs for platinum albums. To big-city clubs. To a recording studio used by the Rolling Stones. And to talk of appearances at museums, other international concerts, radio, and TV shows.

Henry Qualls, whose music is the distilled essence of the calloused country life he lives, was on the verge of going to the city in a big way.

It could be 1934, the year Henry Qualls was born into an East Texas world where black men were constantly told that they were less than men. Where he grew up with stories of lynchings. Where, when he was seven years old, a white mob broke into a jail in nearby Pittsburg and castrated two black men. Where Henry Qualls learned that a man would be better served to keep to himself. For now, on this cool night—like any cool night in 1934—the only thing that really matters is keeping warm. Keeping warm and playing music while the trains thunder outside the door. The old Texas and Pacific tracks stab right through the middle of Elmo, which is about forty miles east of Dallas and has been Henry Qualls's home since birth. Those restless tracks sit just a few yards from the front door of his 100-year-old house, a place that once belonged to the railroad.

Daryl, one of Henry's ten children, is busy hauling in armloads of gnarly oak. In a center room of the yellow house, Henry has created his own heating system: an abandoned oil drum attached to the fireplace and set on bricks laid atop the weathered floorboards. Henry pries its top open so that Daryl can feed it the new logs. Against the wall leans a bruised guitar. Henry has a name for the instrument, which he bought from Montgomery Ward in 1958: Maybelline. Over the years, he has personalized it, the way people who name their guitars sometimes do. There is a cracked piece of mirror on it; there is a piece of metal, lifted from a car, that reads "Marquis." Qualls, coiled and compact, sits in a rickety metal chair. The dirty boot on his right foot slowly begins scraping, in time, across the floor. Voices ebb, and he waves one hand, his fingers like sticks from a tree. Once in a while, he will caress his pharaoh's beard as if he is coaxing some secret knowledge out of it.

"I used to try and sing the spirituals. I used to think that was the thing I really wanted to do," he preaches as he cradles the guitar and the empty hot-sauce bottle that he uses for a slide. "Then I picked up on Maybelline and started singing the blues. You know, I'm proud of it. Nobody sings to me like she do."

For the rest of the night and into the morning, Henry Qualls presses his guitar to his chest and tells me the story of his life in a voice as worn as rocks in the Red River. He sings those spirituals—the backbone of his existence—that have rarely been heard since the clapboard churches left over from the huge plantations began to collapse. He sings drop-dead-with-sweat songs, some of them his own, that were brewed in the painful Texas and Louisiana farmlands where he and his family stooped for years. There are freedom songs about hopping the trains running from Shreveport to Dallas; Henry lives in a part of Elmo that locals call Frog, because people grew up learning how to jump on and off those freight cars. There are other songs: A thumping, fat-bass boom about love affairs under the illicit silk blanket of darkness. A hip-dipping saga about big-legged women as tasty as country hams. And a getaway sermon about sly rural Romeos making their play and being gone, gone, gone like turkeys through the corn.

It is American music from the 1940s. First-generation music. The music that he learned to play from the people who invented it, in East Texas. The men and women who, at the turn of the century, converted field chants, prison work songs, spirituals, and straight-from-Africa music into what has become known as the country blues. He doesn't stop until seven in the morning. He doesn't stop until the pans of East Texas hot links are empty. Until the friends and other musicians who have stopped by to jam have stumbled away, drunk and exhausted.

Today, in an era when most people who sing country have never been there, Henry Qualls might be one of the last close-to-the-source country-blues musicians in America. It worked out that way for plenty of reasons: He doesn't have a telephone and doesn't want one. He still likes to listen to his thick, clunky 78-rpm records. For him, music worth listening to—worth playing—ceased being made back when President Truman was running things up in Washington.

He would pick up his guitar for a few years and then put it down for a few years. He played for himself and, sometimes, at an occasional house party, where someone would fire up a barbecue, pass around homemade beer and moonshine, and tell stories all night long. He played music the way he lived: for himself, for his family, for his friends. "I'm not into music to make money," he tells me one night as the sun is disappearing outside his door. "I started playing spirituals because my grandmother liked them. You know, I've done lots of jobs. I'm a mechanic. I mow fields. I build things."

Now, he is slumped into a grimy easy chair. There is a rack of ribs in the kitchen that needs chopping. He watches the flames inside that oil drum in his living room. "Man, that music can be the hardest job in the world," he tells me. It is one of the few times that he has become reflective around people who aren't his family. "I've always just played music for fun. Well, I guess I'll go overseas. We'll see what happens."

It is late on a Saturday night, and coyotes have cocked their heads back and aimed them at a fertile East Texas moon. The howls ripple across the moist fields and float in the direction of Elmo, a town that doesn't make many maps. Right now, a battered pickup truck is heading in the same direction, kicking rocks alongside a pockmarked road. Henry Qualls is coming home after a day of pushing through the bushes and piney woods. He has his old rifle in his lap, one hand on the wheel, and the other wrapped around a bottle of mouth-puckering whiskey that he gets from a nearby bootlegger. There were no wild hogs. Not even a squirrel, possum, or coon.

This is how he survives. This is what comes before his music—this is what informs his music. To understand his sound, he says, you must first understand how he lives and how he feels about both the city and the country: "Let me tell you how poor folks live," he begins to bark as he parks alongside a 1949 tractor nestled next to the venerable yellow house. Henry bought the building with the money he made from mowing farmers' fields—as well as the lawns of the fine expensive homes in the uptown neighborhoods of Dallas. There have been, since he was born, only three things Henry Qualls has come to the city for: To see his mother. To soak up the style of the original roots musicians of Texas—Lightnin' Hopkins, Lil' Son Jackson, Frankie Lee Sims—played in low-ceilinged juke joints and dice halls in the Trinity River bottomlands. And, he hisses at me, "to mow rich people's yards."

Nothing ever pleased Henry Qualls more than to see the skyline of Dallas disappearing in his rearview mirror. The quicker the miles clicked by, the easier he could breathe. The closer he got to Elmo, the more he felt like a free man. Henry's family traces back to southern Louisiana, where his grandmother was a cook before she followed the cotton-picking trail to Texas. His mother moved from the Elmo area to South Dallas long ago. His wife packed up and went to the city a few years ago. When they left the country, they left behind the deep country ways: Wrapping turnip greens in heated rags to cure frostbite. Sipping some noxious tea with pinches of dried "cow chips" in it. Using the bitter green persimmon to improve a woman's sex life.

Tonight, the city is the furthest thing from Henry's mind. Tonight in Elmo, under the moonlight, you can see two deep furrows permanently snaking across his forehead. His beard is the color of dirty snow. His eyes are like almonds behind frosted glass. Henry says he can live, as he has for a good chunk of his sixty-plus years, off the East Texas earth that is as black as an old lady's funeral dress. In the area around his small parcel of land, there are things to eat, things that few people in the cities have heard about. Sour dot weeds. Pepper weeds. Muscadine grapes. Black hull. Wild pears. There are even alligators out there, like the eight-foot one that his buddy Brown just pulled from the pond.

"I don't have to buy anything," Henry tells me, his voice a batch of rusty nails in a can. "I can just . . . live."

Henry Qualls never really cared about taking his guitar to town. He never thought much about singing to city folks about getting back to the country. And his unexpected trip to Europe was something he never invited. It began with two white guys who first met on the late-evening Texas music circuit. The two kept seeing each other at club after club, night after night, until they realized they were following the same blues-head beat. Scotty Ferris was a former heavy-metal musician who underwent a Saul-on-the-road-to-Damascus conversion after hearing Oak Cliff's Stevie Ray Vaughan play a Stratocaster. He was living in East Texas, working at the huge Wal-Mart photo-processing plant in Terrell, and spending more time in blues joints than his wife really liked. Chuck Nevitt was a burly ex–cab driver who grew up in the same Oak Cliff neighborhood as Stevie Ray Vaughan, kept his ear glued to the black radio stations, and was earning a reputation as a one-man encyclopedia of Texas blues. A few years ago, he walked away from the dangerous days and nights of cabbing and began devoting more time to his Dallas Blues Society, which he founded in the 1980s to promote grassroots music, share research, and put on blues shows. He turned his passion into a serious business in 1987, when he rediscovered a big-voiced 1950s recording star who for thirty years had been living anonymously in Dallas flophouses and earning a meager wage pressing pants.

The Dallas Blues Society man emptied his slim bank account to coax that singer, Zuzu Bollin, into the studio and onto festival stages here and abroad. The record was praised in *Rolling Stone*, and Zuzu Bollin was featured on the covers of music magazines in the United States and Europe. But almost as quickly as Zuzu Bollin's career reignited, he succumbed in 1990 to years of booze, crack, and countless unfiltered cigarettes. Chuck Nevitt lost a friend—and all of his money. He told people, including Scotty Ferris, that there would be no next time. God would have to come to earth with a guitar before he would agree to do what he had done for Zuzu Bollin.

Then, two years ago, a truck driver passing through the Wal-Mart plant in Terrell saw Ferris's Dallas Blues Society T-shirt.

"Man, there's an old guy who lives in a big yellow house by the tracks that you oughta go hear," he said.

The photo-processing blues player made a mental note to check it out. Many months later, he finally headed down the rutted dirt road alongside the railroad tracks in Elmo. Henry Qualls was waiting for him. He was suspicious of the lean, long-haired white guy. He said he didn't play music anymore. Nonetheless, the white blues player invited the old man out to his East Texas spread to mess around on some guitars. It seemed, he thought, as though Henry Qualls had a lot locked up inside his head. Over the next several months, the layers peeled away. Henry enjoyed hanging out with people half his age who loved the music he grew up with in the 1930s and 1940s. The old man brought out Maybelline. He began working backward, chronologically, historically, and musically. He began inviting the white blues player and a handful of other North Texas musicians to the yellow house. In time, there was music every Saturday night in Henry Qualls's living room or on the muddy ground between his house and the tracks.

He covered some B. B. King songs that every blues bar band has yawned through. There were some semiobscure Jimmy Reed tunes. There were seldom-heard tunes and riffs from Texas musicians who perfected the state's rural blues sound. Then there were the things that only hard-core blues freaks knew: Lil' Son Jackson songs that came right from the rich earth around Tyler, songs that were wedded to the beginnings of recorded music. And, finally, there were the things that no one had ever heard: the spirituals, the personal songs, the tales from one black man's life in East Texas. Scotty Ferris finally made a wobbly videotape of Henry Qualls from Elmo, Texas, and gave it to his friend in Dallas.

Chuck Nevitt, who had invested his soul and his life savings in Zuzu Bollin, was still telling friends that he would never do it again. He had lost a lot, financially and emotionally. With Zuzu, he had learned to be producer, manager, nurse, roadie, priest, chauffeur, critic, friend, and, finally, undertaker. But as he stared at the videotape of Henry Qualls—the old country-blues singer effortlessly summoning up pieces of Texas musical history—he was changing his mind. He watched in silent amazement and played the tape over and over.

"I knew that the last guy to be discovered who played this kind of stuff was Mance Lipscomb," Nevitt told me. Navasota, Texas, native Lipscomb, considered by most musicologists to be one of the cornerstones of American music, was born in 1895 and wasn't "discovered" and put on a record until 1960. Nevitt decided to do exactly what he had done with Zuzu Bollin. He was ready to sink what little money he had—money he had been making by selling stereo equipment he bought at garage sales—in the old man with the guitar named Maybelline. He anted up several thousand dollars to rent studio time, to hire engineers, to produce some songs, to take out ads, and to sell some music.

The morning after watching the videotape, he drove straight to Elmo and offered Henry Qualls—who had never seen the inside of a recording studio, who was still listening to 78 records—the chance to cut an album and travel to clubs around the country and in Europe. Posters began going up around Dallas announcing that Henry "House Party" Qualls—"Texas Blues Discovery of the Year!"—was going to be featured for the first time.

Qualls agreed to see where it would all take him. The blues-bar showcase was just one of the performance dates being arranged. Nevitt also was booking studio time and playing his Elmo tape for those foreign promoters who catered to the wide, still-growing audiences for real American blues.

Now, Henry sat to one side of J&J Blues Bar with a posse of friends from Elmo and watched as the place filled with young white faces. By show time, Henry was deep into his bootleg beverage. Wannabe white players who had come to the show after hearing the buzz about Henry through the blues grapevine slid more free drinks into his hand. Nevitt nervously asked Henry whether he was OK. "Man, we're gonna murder them," he replied.

Then, in the middle of a warm-up act by a belter from Fort Worth named Lady Pearl Johnson, the house-party musician from Elmo, Texas—the man who had mowed fields and lawns for most of his life—inexplicably walked on stage. He reached for a microphone and began singing a spiritual. The band from Fort Worth looked as if it was ready to rumble. A nervous energy clicked through the crowd. I watched as Scotty and Chuck carefully, gingerly, lured Henry back down.

Close to midnight, this time on cue, he took the stage again: "I've got to put God into everything I do," announced Henry, staring out at the sea of strangers. His voice thick with liquor and his hands tumbling across the strings, the normally chilling spirituals were lost in the laughter and din of the cavernous club. He seemed to grow more nervous as he stumbled, yelling out fragments and shards: "That old ship of Zion, that old ship of Zion."

Finally, after several awkward minutes, Scottie pulled the plug from Henry's amplifier. It was a bad, painful night. And watching it all come down, Chuck thought to himself: This was the first white crowd he had ever played for. The biggest and the whitest.

A drink in his hand, Henry Qualls slumped into his seat after leaving the stage. Laughing, he lit up cigarette after cigarette and stared hard at each act that followed him.

A month later, Qualls is sitting on a folding chair deep inside the Sumet Sound Studios. The North Dallas studio is, for some people, an intimidating place. The Rolling Stones, ZZ Top, James Brown, and Merle Haggard have recorded here. Henry sucks on a cigarette, and the smoke envelops his head. Sound engineer Bob Sullivan, someone who once worked with Elvis Presley, punches buttons, moves microphones, and checks sound levels. Chuck Nevitt and Scotty Ferris watch from behind the thick glass separating them from Qualls. For the next six hours, the tape rolls, and Henry is on the money. Again and again, he puts a flame to another smoke, kicks his feet at the softly carpeted floor, slides his hot-sauce bottle up and down the strings—and another East Texas stomp is in the bag. It is, the veteran sound engineer whispers, just like the old times. Like the days when Elvis, Buddy Holly, and all the others were first starting out. It is, the engineer says with a knowing smile, like when a performer was booked into a studio for one day only and had to churn out a dozen songs. Back then, the songs were cranked out without any overdubbing or any of the months-long multitrack editing, cutting, and pasting that every recording has these days.

On short breaks, Henry touches a bottle of Eight Star whiskey to his lips and talks about the last time he came to Dallas—and the crash and burn in Deep Ellum. "Man, I ain't gonna do that again," he mutters. "Nobody is going to tell me what to do. But I appreciate what people are doing for me. I ain't gonna let that happen again. No, sir," says Henry as he raises his whiskey bottle. Out of those Eight Stars, at least six, maybe seven, have fallen.

In the control room, the sound engineer has rewound the master tapes. Henry's songs seep out of the huge speakers and into the acoustically perfect recording studio. It is a bottomless sound. A heavy sound that is part prayer, part feast. Then a booming voice. Henry Qualls shakes his head, runs a hand through his ancient beard, and I watch him as he breaks into thunderclaps of raspy, rattling laughter.

Curiosity about Henry Qualls snaked through the North Texas network, down to Austin, and out to California. The drummer for West Coast bluesman Charlie Musselwhite made the trek to Elmo to play with Henry. Antone's, the legendary blues club in Austin, was interested. And word about Henry Qualls danced across Europe, where the roots music of America, from jazz to blues, is often held in higher esteem than in the place where it was born. Articles were published about him in Holland and Britain, and then there was that matter of the music festival. Japp Hendrix, the Dutch producer who has orchestrated the Utrecht Blues Festival for fifteen years, has only one musician penciled in—Henry Qualls.

"It was so exciting to hear that music," he tells me, several weeks after the tape was played for him over the phone. "It's not common anymore, that original roots American music. I had to hire him on the spot."

Tony Burke, editor of England's influential *Blues & Rhythm—The Gospel Truth*, says Henry Qualls will be on his magazine's cover. He heard the same cassette tape that Hendrix did. "There's no doubt about it. What will happen when the CD is issued is that there will be a great deal of interest among all these blues fans," says Burke. "Henry Qualls carries on the tradition of the great Texas bluesmen like Lightnin' Hopkins and especially Lil' Son Jackson. I mean, along comes Henry Qualls, who keeps alive the best of the Texas country-blues tradition. There's already a tremendous interest, and I'm sure he'll come over to Europe."

Dick Waterman, the Mississippi-based musicologist, manager, and producer who was one of the first to hear the Henry Qualls tape, has worked closely with blues founding fathers and founding daughters, such as Bonnie Raitt. He says that the possibility of someone playing relatively unfettered country blues is stunning. "To find someone who has had, at least, some level of being in a semivacuum—who hasn't been bombarded with all these outside musical influences—is extraordinary," he says, speaking from his home in Oxford, Mississippi, not far from the Delta region where B. B. King, Muddy Waters, Robert Johnson, and dozens of other pivotal players were born. "It's clear from listening to the tape that Henry has rejected modern influences and that he has simply been a man who enjoys his own company, his own music."

But Henry Qualls's future is less clear: "He has never had to have his musical limitations tested or extended. He has never been professionally tested," says the Mississippi musicologist. "I wonder what he'll do. If a guy is taking the money that he makes back into a rural setting, is he going to spend it on kerosene, lard, and rolling papers? Will he bring it back to rural Texas?"

On a clear, cold Saturday afternoon, Nevitt has gone to Elmo to keep Henry posted on possible club dates, the record release, and the trip to Europe. Because Henry still refuses to get a phone, whenever the producer needs to talk to him, he has to drive out to the yellow house. The producer has news about the future: the cover photographs are almost ready—taken by a photographer who has done dozens of albums for well-known artists including Anita Baker, Dwight Yoakum, Michael Franks, and even Boy George. The liner notes are being written. Special decals—ones that read "Hotter Than A Pot Of Neckbones"—are being prepared to put on the compact-disc case.

But today Henry seems to be staying clear of me and the future. He is dancing around all those questions: Will he bring it all back to Elmo? What will happen to him if he has to leave the country? Right now, this day, all he wants to do is talk to me about the old days, and about how the only thing he is looking forward to is another Saturday-night jam session inside his railroad house. Scotty will play bass. Another guitar player named Dale will be there. Son Daryl will play drums. They will play all night long, until Henry hops into his pickup truck as the sun rises and bumps down the road with his rifle by his side.

"Old Man Emmit Williams was the one who taught me how to play," Henry tells me as he stamps his feet to keep out the cold. A couple of buddies—including Clarence Brown, the farmer who roped the eight-foot alligator—are hanging out with him.

"My grandmother said, 'You'd never amount to much if you play that starvation box.'" Henry giggles at his grandmother's description of a guitar. Henry will talk about the future only as it affects others. Like his half brother out there somewhere: no one knows whether he is alive or dead. Henry thinks it could be the latter, and he suspects that the half brother might have been swallowed up by the shadows in the big city. "They're crazy down there. People can't remember their own name in the city. There's bodies all down by the river in the city. They put bodies down there; it's a good place for that," he says, his voice thick with disgust.

Henry lets loose another sandpaper laugh and circles the ancient, but still operating, water well. It sits in his side yard, near the patch of land where his muscadine grapes come up every year. Suddenly there is a plodding, insistent rumble. From behind the trees, a long iron monster thunders into view. The wind from the freight train blows little clouds of East Texas dirt as it hurtles alongside Henry Qualls's shuddering house. Like all the other trains that have been passing by today, it is steaming toward the big city. When the last car roars away, there is a big silence.

"You got to know what to do if you want to hop that train," Henry says.

Qualls's record was released to critical acclaim. He played at festivals and clubs in Texas and in Europe. He still hated going into Dallas. He was stunned, like most bluesmen, by the adoration he received from people outside the United States. He died in December 2003, at the age of sixty-nine. He never moved from his home in Elmo, Texas. After he died, friends pooled their money to get him a nice headstone. It had a picture of Henry playing his guitar. Underneath the picture, engraved in the stone, it read: "HENRY AND MAYBELLINE." On the bottom of the stone, it read: "PRECIOUS LORD TAKE MY HAND."

LIGHTNIN' BLUES

Not long after I moved to Houston, Lightnin' Hopkins passed. I had learned that people simply said someone had "passed"—not died or passed away. Passed. The same way that people said they "stayed" somewhere when they wanted to tell you where they lived. People "stayed" in Dallas or Houston or San Antonio. And when they died, they "passed." I decided to go to his memorial service. There really wasn't much choice. He was an immortal, and he was headed to the blues Valhalla. Music fans draw up lists all the time. I didn't know much, never would, but I knew that Hopkins was on the final list. I had seen the old photographs, buried in the newspaper morgue, that showed him with his hair pomaded, his sunglasses on, his hat tilted at some angle. I had written about him years earlier. He was irascible, a hustler, a keeper of stories, and when he played, it was an error to be lulled by his expert effortlessness, lulled to the point that you didn't really hear what he was saying. He made painful truths so plain and easy to see. At the funeral home, he looked the same way he did while he lived—sharp, hip, sly. A young white woman was there with a big-time attorney, and she asked me whether I would walk toward the body with her. I did. There were people singing in a nearby lot. There were bottles being passed around.

I thought about sitting near Muddy Waters's family one time in the Delta, on one of his first and only gigs back home after he had gotten really famous. His relatives—aunts, uncles, cousins, siblings—had come up from Rolling Fork to Greenville. They were sitting in folding chairs, in a cotton field, and listening to McKinley Morganfield, aka Muddy Waters, on his trip back home. It was like that in Houston the night Hopkins was laid out. It was as though his family had gathered, in his house, and people moved from room to room, sharing stories, cool beverages, music. He looked, for sure, as if he were taking it all in.

The man with the sunglasses and the 1977 black Cadillac Coupe de Ville was a fixture in the Third Ward. And everybody in the neighborhood around Gray Street used to treat him with respect. It might have had to do with the fact that he preferred to live there instead of in his house in the Sunnyside area. Or it might have had to do with the fact that he was always dressed to kill—often in a suit, his head capped with a fine new hat. Perhaps it might have been because he had once been in the same room with the queen of England—and that she had been in that room just to see him and not vice versa. Whatever, he had the respect of a lot of people.

"Now . . . he came in here every day," Dorothy Rice tells me, at the Ralston No. 4 liquor store on McGowen Street. "And every day he'd get a half pint of C&C. That was his drink. We'll miss Mr. Hopkins."

"Mr. Hopkins," the blues musician better known as Lightnin', died two days before the beginning of Black History Month, of pneumonia brought on by cancer. He had been in St. Joseph Hospital, not too far from the corners where he used to hang out. And the neighborhood turned out on a chilly Tuesday at Johnson's Funeral Chapel, on McGowen, to pay its respects. At seven, an hour before the announced memorial service was set to begin, I joined the crowd filling the street. Cars were being parked three blocks away, and the hundreds of mourners, most of them black, formed a single line that curled around the corner of the chapel. Security officers let four or five people in at a time, and they dutifully joined another line inside the building as they waited to sign the visitors' book. Inside the small room with the open coffin, there were several guitar-shaped wreaths. His immediate family— four children and his wife, Antoinette—sat to one side.

They looked on as a diverse set of people came through the door: bluesman Amos Milburn's brother Garcia, who runs a classic blues club up in the Heights; Rocky Hill, a white bluesman and the brother of ZZ Top's Dusty Hill; big-time defense attorney Jimmy Baker; a young black bluesman known as Little Rose; and, wearing a neat pinstriped suit from the Duke of Hollywood store downtown, the reclusive leader of ZZ Top, Billy Gibbons. There were hundreds more who claimed to have known Hopkins, including dozens who remembered him from his early days in East Texas. Hill had known Hopkins for years. As the night went on, as people swapped stories and beverages, he stood outside the chapel as the clock pressed toward nine. He watched the people still filing in, he watched the cops direct traffic. Hill had brought along his guitar. "He was like a Picasso," Hill tells me.

The line never seems to end. It looks as if the funeral home will be open a long, long time. In the parking lot, some people are singing. There is a bottle

being passed around. Amos Milburn's brother tells me that I better come see him tomorrow at his club. Hill plays a blues song on his guitar. And Lightnin' is laid out nice and fine, sunglasses on, floating on a sea of silk, the air thick with the smell of cut flowers and sweating men and tangy cologne. Hill is playing some quiet blues run, and the sound is mixing with the scrape of feet along the wooden floor. The one thing about Lightnin' was that, even if he wanted to cut you, he always seemed to be smiling. You couldn't read him too well, because his eyes were always behind the big sunglasses and his hat was tipped down low. It was a perfect look, really—perfect for stealing a glance at something always out of reach, for casting a spell or even a hex on someone or something that needed, deserved to be tamed and maybe put to rest. When he was alive, he looked as if he were having the last laugh. In his coffin, he looked the same damned way. He was, in his way, a creature of habit. Lightnin' could keep real good time. He could see you even if you couldn't see him.

Lightnin' was your friend, for a while, if you wanted to roll the bones. Other legendary bluesmen and close friends such as Muddy Waters would come to visit and jam. And if he could do it, he would entice visitors into a game of craps, something he was ready to play anytime, anywhere, even out in the streets. "He was shooting craps until he died," is what Dr. Cecil Harold, Hopkins's manager and physician, tells me when I go to see him one day at his South Houston office.

The dice aside, the people who saw him hanging out on the corners of Delano, Gray, and McGowen remember Hopkins as a quiet, polite man, someone who probably didn't have a firm grip on how influential his music had been. He was one of the most important roots musicians in American history, and he never really wanted to do more than be on the corner with his friends, his pints, his guitar, and his dice. "He lived in the neighborhood for years and years. He was always a gentleman. He wore a jacket, a nice pair of slacks. Everybody knew who he was, and everybody treated him with respect," says Miss Rice at the liquor store.

That respect might have been born out of deference to the blues that he lived and then sang about. Born March 15, 1912, in the East Texas town of Centerville, he picked up a guitar when he was seven, began to play for money when he was a teenager, and then began to "hobo around." "He was the baby of the family," Harold told me that day I sat in his medical office, not far from where Hopkins kept a house for Antoinette and the four children. "You know, they used to say that his older brother, John Henry, was a better guitar player. Lightnin's father got killed when he was three, so he was always roaming around."

At fourteen, Sam Hopkins—he acquired the name "Lightnin'" in 1946 when he teamed with pianist Thunder Smith for an Aladdin Records session in Los Angeles—met up with Jabo Buck, a legendary East Texas fiddle player. They traveled from Navasota to Buffalo, Texas, and began to play in front of a bar. After a few tunes, they were invited inside, and Hopkins had his first paying gig. From there, he hit a string of Texas towns: Jewitt, Crockett, and Palestine. "I'd say from the age of fifteen into his forties, he was always traveling around the country. He'd pick pecans and play at a dance on a weekend and make six dollars. It was hard. He used to hop trains all over the place," Harold told me.

And no matter where he sang—the raunchiest honky-tonk in Leland, Mississippi, or the famous clubs of Houston, including McDaniel's, Liberty Hall, The Palace, and The Bronze Peacock—Hopkins always included one particular song in his set: "When the Saints Go Marching In." It was his mother's favorite song. In the middle of any one of his songs about chain gangs, jealous husbands, or deadly women, Hopkins would sneak in a few bars of "Saints" on his guitar. After his musical tribute to his mother, he would segue right back into his original song. Harold knew it all the time: "Lightnin' lived the blues until the day he died. A lot of blacks in Texas and all over lived the same blues. But Lightnin' was able to put it into music and song. And he could do it in a way that would get your attention. He wrote a lot of social commentary."

There was "Blues for John Glenn," written for the astronaut when the nation watched him and the space program. But most of all, Hopkins sang about things he knew firsthand: "Coffee Blues," "Short Haired Woman," "Big Mama Jump!" "River Stay Away from My Door," and "Penitentiary Blues." That last one was inspired by a stint Hopkins did in jail and then on a road gang after being busted for gambling.

As Harold unfolded Hopkins's history for me, he leaned back in his chair and pointed at his phone: "You know that Lightnin' never had one of those until he got sick. If there was anything he hated, it was being interviewed by the press, TV, radio. That posed a lot of problems for me. Lightnin' had a unique way of understanding only what he wanted to understand, when he wanted." Exasperation was creeping all over Harold's voice. When people wanted Hopkins to come to their big festivals in New York or Europe, Harold would have to hop in his car, drive downtown, and pull the musician away from the things he loved in the Third Ward. And in the car they would debate the merits of the gig. And finally the doctor would head to a nearby pay phone and would call Paris or Amsterdam to give them Lightnin' Hopkins's answer.

Harold endured it, because he knew what everyone else knew. Hopkins was the poet laureate of the streets, and the oral historian, in his way, of all those things and people that flowed from East Texas into the big city. They had met, almost incongruously, when Hopkins played a show in the 1960s at the Jewish Community Center in Houston. He knew that Hopkins could put into words the words of a black community that seemed to still be reeling from the Great Depression. From all those ghosts that ran through the East Texas woods and came streaming into Houston, Texas. In time, Harold came to realize something about the genius mind of Lightnin' Hopkins: "He had a unique problem. He would only remember the things he wanted to remember."

In his coffin, in the weak light of the funeral home in the Third Ward, Lightnin' Hopkins looked as if he were remembering exactly what he wanted to remember. Anything else would tip him off the main track, anything else would probably have roared up alongside him and laid him down to sleep a long, long time ago.

"The life I'm living, I've been living it for a many year / . . . I know the chariot was coming for me but I didn't know / What kind of chariot gonna take me away from here."

One of his guitars is on display at the Rock and Roll Hall of Fame, and many people assume it is only a matter of time before he is inducted. One musicologist suggested that no blues musician released more records than Hopkins, a testimony to his popularity and importance. "Rolling Stone" put him on its list of the 100 greatest guitarists of all time.

CHICKEN SHACK BLUES

I met Garcia Milburn at Lightnin' Hopkins's memorial service. He was standing in line behind me. He told me I didn't know anything if I didn't know about his brother. He told me I had to come to his club. I did, and it became a place that I visited more than any other in Houston. The best musicians in Texas would stop in, unannounced, just to hang out. Sometimes to jam. Albert Collins would come by all the time. They came out of respect for the legacy of Amos Milburn, they came for the hospitality of his brother Garcia. It was profoundly sad, sitting with Milburn as he talked about his brother. It was as if Amos embodied the entire history of oversight, neglect. His brother was a legend with a huge following, but where was the recognition? What would it take?

Garcia introduced me to some members of his family. He told me he was going to name one of his roosters "Billy." We talked on the phone, our conversations consisting mainly of my asking him for advice, asking for directions, asking about music. Like a lot of things, longevity and commitment helped: I spent a lot of money and time at his place. He came to my apartment by the Fourth Ward. He wasn't a musician, not in the way his brother was, but he cared deeply about the music and about his brother's memory. There really wasn't anything in it for him. He just wanted people to know that his brother had left his mark on Mother Earth. I knew he really wanted me to answer this question: "Was that too much too ask?" I'm glad he never directly posed it that way to me. I still didn't know anything about the blues. How could I?

It is ten on a Monday night—"Blue Monday," as it is called at Garcia Milburn's club on 33rd Street, down the block from Main Street in Houston, Texas. Milburn is, well a little bent out of shape. He is sucking on a straw, the straw nestled between some chunks of ice in a plastic cup. The cup is filled with J&B. In the background, in a corner of the older wooden building, the members of the Triple Threat Band are cueing into "Satin Doll." The people in the band—including the trumpet player, who just got his horn out of hock—have played with everybody from Ray Charles to B. B. King. Ray Charles had told me that whenever he put a band together, he always looked for musicians from Houston. I walked in on Charles one night in the back room of an old Houston bank that had been converted into a club. He had just finished his set, and when I tiptoed into the room, I saw him staring down at a chessboard. He was playing chess, by himself, which seemed to make sense. Ray Charles could do whatever he wanted, anytime he wanted. Without looking up, he said: "I was wondering when you were going to get here." I wasn't sure what he meant. We had talked a bit on the phone in the past, but that was about it. Ray Charles knew things about Houston; that is all I really knew.

And back at that club on 33rd, where Ray's musicians liked to gather, I could see Garcia filling with anger: "It's a damn shame. Not only was my brother a great musician, he was a great man. Ask anybody out there," says Garcia, waving his hand in the general direction of the street.

On a tabletop in front of Garcia are some albums with yellowing covers. Staring out from them, his hair neatly processed, is a man with a wide smile, raised eyebrows, and what could pass for a pencil-thin moustache: piano player extraordinaire and R&B great Amos Milburn. The anniversary of Milburn's death had just passed. Two years earlier, in 1980, Amos had died. One leg amputated, his fast hands frozen with paralysis. There wasn't much of a fuss. No television crews. No reporters. A few musicians came—and so did a lot of black people who also had yellowing albums in their homes.

But for the most part, Milburn went quietly—uncharacteristically quietly. After all, this was the Amos Milburn who used to drive around downtown Houston in a chartreuse Cadillac, tossing silver dollars as he roared by. "That boy is crazy," some whites would say. "Some day we'll get him." But they rarely ever got Amos Milburn.

It is a hot day in the early 1950s. The hummable little song that Sam Cooke later made famous—"Chain Gang"—is a reality for lots of people. A lot of people in Texas and throughout the South. A chartreuse Caddy tools along a dusty Texas road. Behind it, a chartreuse bus is kicking up dirt as it speeds along. On the side of the bus, in big fancy letters, is written "Amos Milburn and His Aladdin Chicken Shackers."

Up ahead, there is a line of people. They are standing abnormally close to one another. When the chartreuse caravan gets closer to the scene, the sun reflects on the chains that bind the legs of the black men.

Amos Milburn reaches down onto the seat of the Cadillac. When he pulls alongside the road gang, he casually flips a pack of cigarettes to the prisoners. He tosses some money. He winks slyly. The bus and the car roll on. The white men with shotguns stare: it is not often they see a black man go by in a chartreuse Caddy, his hair slicked back and a big diamond on his finger.

"Was Amos important?" The question is posed to me by the legendary Houston saxophone player Don Wilkerson, who went on the road and into the recording studio with Milburn. Wilkerson knows—he knows everything, just like Ray Charles. Wilkerson took solos on some of Charles's most important songs. He was the kind of musician, straight out of Houston, that Charles called for. "Well, let me put it this way. You couldn't consider, say, the late 1940s up through the early 1950s without including him." You couldn't consider those years, musically speaking, without mentioning Milburn. He was, perhaps, the biggest-selling black artist of his time.

His tall brother Garcia, perhaps a little biased, puts it this way to me: "He was bigger than anybody in their prime. I mean, he was bigger than people like Fats Domino."

Bigger or not, Milburn was a legend in the black community, a legend for his music and his lifestyle. During his heyday, roughly 1948–1953, the left-handed pianist traveled with his band from coast to coast, playing his version of R&B and boogie-woogie before sold-out audiences. In New York, he appeared at the famous palace of black entertainment, the Apollo Theater. He did guest stints at clubs on 52nd Street, then the jazz headquarters of the world. He played at the Savoy, Avalon, Five-Four, and other then-big clubs across the country.

After hours, Milburn rubbed elbows, shared drinks, and made music with Duke Ellington, Dizzy Gillespie, and Nat King Cole. His records, they were called "race records" back then, were selling: "Chicken Shack Boogie"; "Bad, Bad Whiskey"; "One Scotch, One Bourbon, One Beer."

He was one of twelve children of a Houston construction worker. Born in 1927, Amos, at the age of fourteen or fifteen, managed to fake his way into the navy. He came out three years later and began to play piano professionally. An older brother and drummer, Frederick, who was steeped in the zydeco-blues music scene, had helped Amos learn the piano, saxophone, and guitar. But Milburn cut his teeth in the bars on Lyons Avenue, when that street was one of the destination spots for black culture in Texas. Everyone knew Lyons Avenue. It was one of the reasons Juke Boy Bonner, another Texas legend, used to sing "Houston . . . man, that's an action town." Bonner sang another song, about staying off Lyons Avenue if you "were green," because there was a chance you would never "be seen."

Milburn knew how to cut it. In 1945, he landed a job with the mad Slam Stewart Trio on a gig in San Antonio at Don Albert's Keyhole Club, a place that quietly made a lot of Texas musical history. It was really Milburn's first big-time break. And he began picking up more work on the Texas club circuit: Texas City, La Marque, Fort Worth, and Dallas. The clubs were often racially integrated. The people in search of the blues, the music, were going to find it. It happened in Harlem, it happened in Texas. By the close of the 1940s, he decided to do what a lot of Texas musicians had done. Instead of following the blues path to Chicago, like the musicians from the Delta did, he followed the trail to Los Angeles, to California, where there were Texas barbecue shacks and all kinds of nods to the Lone Star State in the wake of a postwar migration. All up and down Central Avenue in LA, you could run into somebody from Texas. T-Bone Walker from Dallas was there. So was Charles Brown from Galveston. And a hundred more, all of them working up their urban blues, their cool blues, putting an elegant sheen on the things that crept out of the East Texas woods. It was a money thing, this matter of going to California, but it was where you could breathe, a little better, without worrying about the way you dressed, the car you drove, the profession you chose. It was dicey, very dicey, to live as a professional musician in some parts of Texas.

In LA, Milburn hooked up with Aladdin, the same label that a friend of his from Houston—Lightnin' Hopkins—was to record for. From 1948 to 1953, Milburn had sixteen songs at or near the top of the R&B charts. At some point in that period, it was safe to say that no one was more important in "race record" circles than Amos Milburn from Houston, Texas.

But like so many black musicians from the same period, Milburn almost just as quickly dropped out of the national spotlight. Rock music was coming. And, of course, so was the ultimate irony: the music he helped create also sealed his fate. Sitting with his brother one night in Houston, I would not have been surprised to see Amos come walking through the door. The music, the building, and so much more had never changed. It was as if the world, everything in it, was an old, yellowing photograph. "It's awful. I won't say that people stole things from him, but a lot of people imitated his style. He was a creator," Garcia tells me.

A creator.

The Triple Threat Band is taking a break. I watch as Garcia dips into one of those faded album covers and pulls out an old disc. The sound is unmistakably his brother's: a rolling piano solo, the left hand pounding out a beefy bass run.

When record companies started looking for white acts, Milburn's backup group disbanded in the mid-1950s. He sang with a variety of bands and even barnstormed across the country as part of the early "rock 'n' roll" caravans that featured several groups on the same bill. But after living in his candy-colored bus and in hotels all across the country, Milburn decided to settle in the black side of town in Cincinnati, and he could be spotted playing in a place called Satan's Den. It was a long way down. Talk reached Houston. Talk that he was missing his piano keys, drinking too much. "His wife had died of cancer, and I went up there and brought him back," Garcia tells me as he fiddles with his straw.

He played a number of clubs in black neighborhoods where time had stood still, and his health began to melt away. He suffered a stroke. He had a leg amputated in 1979. His hands—which Wilkerson says were as fast as anybody's in the business—wouldn't do what he wanted them to do. Six months after he lost a leg and had been exiled to a wheelchair, Milburn died.

Quietly.

"The music business is very fickle," Wilkerson is telling me. "It makes no difference who you are. Now, Amos had quite a few imitators. After his big period, the white R&B bands took the format." Wilkerson pauses a bit to see whether I can even remotely understand. "He had an ethnic band, if you know what I mean. It was meant for blacks."

An ethnic band.

At Garcia's, the scratchy record is still spinning.

Amos Milburn is singing, plaintive but urgent, about his self-medicating conundrum, about how he tries . . . and tries again . . . but can't seem to fly right. How he has to have something to make sense of it all. How he walks with two angels on his shoulder, the risen one and the fallen one. He tried milk and water, but he knows something will make him shift to something stronger: "Milk and water, milk and water . . . / Don't get me wrong, I won't be on this kick for long."

His brother watches the Triple Threat Band, one of the musical ties that bind Texas to Amos Milburn and everything he stands for. They're getting ready for another Blue Monday set. It could be Satan's Den. "I wanted to be something, like my brother. I wanted to have that money. He used to sing 'All I want for Christmas is a chartreuse Cadillac and a diamond ring.' You know, he didn't value his money. He could have bought up Houston, but he used to give it away."

I can see the money floating out of that chartreuse Cadillac, floating out into the hot Texas wind and flying away, flying toward the outstretched hands of the chain gang working to build that new road from Houston to Dallas . . . I can see the money flapping and being reflected in the mirrored sunglasses of the prison guards. I can see a hand with a diamond ring sliding back inside the car, the window rolling up and that car fading fast.

Garcia stands and takes the record off the turntable, carefully replacing it in its jacket. Sitting back on his bar stool, Garcia tells me this: "You know, Amos always had a religious background. He knew how to have fun, but he was religious deep inside. He seemed to lead a better life when he got back to Houston. He used to play the piano at the Right Grove Baptist Church."

Garcia looks away and nods hello to a guitar player coming to jam with all those heirs, standard bearers, stalwarts, potentates, night diviners, and blues mystics who channel everything about Amos Milburn and the earth music in Texas.

In 2000, Garcia asked his son to start a campaign to preserve Amos Milburn's legacy. Various musical organizations, fan clubs, and Web sites have tried to rally efforts to elect Amos Milburn to the Rock and Roll Hall of Fame, especially as a progenitor of rock music. Musicologists and fans like to debate which song was the first "rock 'n' roll recording." Some contend that it was Amos Milburn's "Chicken Shack Boogie." His piano work, his subject matter, influenced many people who decided to make music their life, including other musical pioneers such as Fats Domino. When you consider his influence and the time period in which he was popular, it is clear that Milburn is in the top tier of musicians in the history of Texas.

FOURTH WARD BLUES

One time, in Houston, I played cards with and lost money to the brilliant a capella group the Persuasions. I used to see them whenever I could. At one show, one of the singers built to a frenzy and then threw his jacket into the front rows. I was about twenty rows back, and I saw hands stab for the jacket and pull it in like it was vanishing into a whirlpool. The band left the stage. A minute or two later, the singer sheepishly reappeared—and asked for his jacket back. He said he had money in the inside pocket. It might have been my money. I got hustled by the Persuasions. They took my money. I didn't really mind. It would make a good story.

And that is the way I felt when I was hanging out with Robert Shaw and Lavada "Dr. Hepcat" Durst. They had traveled wide and far. And by the time I went to a small but comfortable home to see them, they had seen enough earnest white musicologists and writers. They had heard the eager questions, the humble entreaties to share some wisdom. And they had to have been a little bemused by it all. Shaw had to be talking about me, inside his sister's house, when he said white people used to be scared. I didn't want to tell him—because I thought he probably knew—that some white people were listening to the music and were still as scared as ever before.

Lavada Durst, better known as Dr. Hepcat, is explaining to me what just happened. "Now, you know, you caught him at just the right moment. Sometimes he doesn't like to deal with strangers," drawls Dr. Hepcat.

"He" is Robert Shaw, grocery man, next-door neighbor, and piano player. He has just finished playing an old standard called "The Ma Grinder," which, depending on how you look at it, is the most obscene song ever conceived. Shaw is wearing a tank-top undershirt, white socks, and black pants, and is sucking on a fat and leafy cigar. His head is bowed, and he is staring down at the Winter piano sitting in the living room of his sister Evelyn's old but neat house on Rosemont, off Scott Street in Houston.

He pulls the cigar out of his mouth and laughs: "Whewwweee. It doesn't make a bit of sense. When I used to play this music in the 1920s and 1930s, white people were scared. They wouldn't come down to the roadhouse to hear me play. They wouldn't be caught near the Fourth Ward. Now, when I look out in the audience, all I see are white faces. Now they can't get enough of it." He pauses and thoughtfully adds: "I guess they learned better."

This last remark elicits a chuckle from Dr. Hepcat; Durst bestowed the name on himself when he was one of the top black deejays in Texas during the 1950s. Durst plays much of the barrelhouse music that Shaw does. He should. He has been learning it from Shaw since they met in 1930.

The bespectacled Shaw, born in 1908, hands his cigar to Evelyn; she is half hiding in the dining room, her chair turned away from the piano but her body leaning toward it. She has a large smile on her face. She is thinking about the fact that back in Stanford, just outside Houston, her little brother Robert used to sneak by the window of the farmhouse and listen to her play the piano. And she is thinking that is how Shaw got started. Started as one of the legion of Houston piano players who specialized in the rolling and stomping mixture of the blues, boogie-woogie, and ragtime that came to be known as roadhouse or barrelhouse music.

"The white folks had what they called clubs. We had the roadsides, or the roadhouses," says Shaw. Those little chicken shacks, where people would tote their food and brew, were all over the Fourth Ward. And they featured the stars of the day: Pegleg Will, Jack Coleman, Rob Cooper, and Boots Walton. Depending on whom you heard, you would catch the big standards of the time: "Black Gal," "Betty Jo," "Sleepin' by Myself," "Hattie Green," and "Put Me in the Alley." Around East Texas, and, for that matter, most of the state, it was understood that some of the best roadside music was coming out of Houston. And to be more specific, out of that stretch of clubs in the Fourth Ward. The area produced a special sound, one that Shaw knew was easily recognizable to anyone who heard it.

Shaw wheels away from me and faces the keyboard again. "Here's the Louisiana style." Out comes a sweet ballad. "Now listen to the Mississippi version." Shaw churns out a choppy blues number: "If you don't believe I'm leaving, then count the days I'm gone."

"You want the Houston style?" He plays an intricate walking-blues number that features some swift left-hand work: "I can see now honey that old train going round and round."

It is what Shaw quit playing for years and years, thinking that as the music got electrified, as blacks got their own "clubs" and the roadside joints went away, it would no longer be appreciated by a wide audience. He retired from the usual means of travel. "I'd be laying out there for the hotshot"—waiting in the bushes and then hopping a fast-moving "hotshot" train headed out of Houston to points north and south. He got into the grocery business in Austin and worked hard. The black chamber of commerce named him the businessman of the year. He played the old music for himself, friends, and relatives, and he played it less and less as he got older. At the same time Shaw was churning out his barbecue in Austin, a Houston folklorist, museum consultant, and cultural historian named Mack McCormick was in the process of trying to track down the music born in the Fourth Ward. He came across the name of Lavada Durst. He traced the disc jockey to Austin and set up a meeting in the early 1960s. When McCormick finally met Durst, the amiable deejay told him the person he really wanted to talk to was Robert Shaw.

McCormick went to Shaw's grocery shop, told the owner that he wanted to know about the old roadside music, and said all signs pointed toward Shaw. After a few noncommittal grunts, Shaw led McCormick out to another building, which had a piano in it. Shaw sat down, still wearing his white apron. He began playing. McCormick, who had spent years combing Texas for original blues music, knew it right away. Shaw's music was perhaps the best living example left of the old Fourth Ward school of music. "He kept it in a pristine state. It was like pulling a picture out of a box. He hadn't been influenced by anyone else. All he knew was the Fourth Ward repertoire."

With McCormick's help, an album was cut, and Shaw slipped back into more regular playing. Shaw traveled the globe visiting blues festivals. He was amazed by it all: "You know, in Europe, they can't understand why people here aren't more crazy about the music."

"I can't think of another city that's produced neighborhood music as unique as that twenty blocks [of the Fourth Ward]," McCormick tells me one day. And when he found Shaw, it was as if Shaw had never really left the Fourth Ward. It was, really, what happened when Louis Armstrong left New Orleans. He never really left it. The Fourth Ward legacy had seeped into

Shaw's marrow. And decades after he had stopped playing, it simply came pouring out.

Shaw stopped riding the trains a long time ago. He travels in an old white 1960 Bonneville that seems to be in excellent shape. And he no longer is involved with the numbers racket: "My job was to keep the bad players off the books. You know, I'd be walkin' around, collecting bets, and there'd be an old woman peeking at me from behind her wash. She'd see me and call me over. 'I had a dream last night,' she'd say. And then she'd give me some money for a bet."

And Shaw doesn't play all night for fifty cents anymore. And he doesn't suffer the indignities and the insults that came from the same people who wouldn't let him eat or play in their clubs: "It was done through meanness. They would look at us as something nasty. But I never got into trouble with those racists. When I met a fool, I'd leave him like that."

Before I leave Evelyn's house, which sits down the block from the Pentecostal Baptist Church, Dr. Hepcat wants to give me something. It is a little bit of patter that Durst, recognized now as one of America's first hip, jive-talking disc jockeys, has penned in honor of his friend and mentor: "Wherever you may travel, from the rock-bound shores of Maine, to the sunny coast of California, from the Eastern states to the Golden Gates, you'll never find another barrelhouse player like Robert Shaw . . . He's as terrific as the Pacific, rougher than the Gulf . . . and tough enough."

In the kitchen, fussing with a bottle of Budweiser, Shaw lets loose a cackle. Soon, he, Evelyn, and Durst are laughing uproariously.

Dr. Hepcat died on Halloween in 1995. Robert Shaw had preceded him in death, in 1985. A few weeks after his death, the Texas Senate honored him with a resolution acknowledging his vast original musical contributions.

ZYDECO
BLUES

I grew up deeply Catholic. My father was a printer, someone who worked with pieces of type, with bars of lead, with an old Heidelberg printing press in our basement. He printed prayer cards with pictures of saints on the front. We called them Italian baseball cards. They were about the same size. He was a good printer; men from the Mafia approached him one time to counterfeit money. He stuck to the Catholic prayer cards and made sure that I became an altar boy. I specialized in serving at funeral masses. I went to dozens of funerals as an altar boy. I learned that people tipped you money at a funeral, but not as much as they tipped you at a wedding. And I went to Catholic school for twelve straight years. All of which did not prepare me for visiting the Catholic-zydeco scene in Houston. I don't know whether it was because I still emitted some altar-boy vibe, or whether it was just the natural balm offered to the wandering stranger who has come out of the desert, but the blues played in the churches, the zydeco-Louisiana-meets-Texas blues that Gatemouth Brown and Clifton Chenier created, was more than welcoming. I found a pay phone in one of the churches and tried to call as many friends around Texas as I could. I was vaguely hoping they would get to me in time. I ate more food, thought about going back to church more often on Sundays, and was one of the last people out. This was gospel, Catholic-zydeco style, and it was definitely not the Latin mass I had celebrated growing up. It was, instead, one of those literally blessed times when the blues came with open arms.

My new best friend, a truly big guy named Big Man, is waving a paw and jabbering in my ear about how "Buckwheat's gotta play me a damn waltz." Big Man offers this thought between noisy polar-bear slurps from a hubcap-sized platter of—God bless and keep her always—Rose Thibodeaux's mighty, mighty gumbo.

Following my instincts regarding any house of worship I have ever visited, I am sitting in the last row of the St. Peter the Apostle church hall on Old Spanish Trail in deepest Houston. It is midnight, and hundreds of hard-backed folding chairs in front of me is Buckwheat Zydeco, a slender, bespectacled musician whose peculiar accordion albatross is to go through life weighed down by the knowledge that he is expected to fill the massive shoes of his mentor, the late Clifton Chenier.

Clifton, who drove refinery trucks in Port Arthur and lived for a long time in Houston, had grown up cutting cane in New Iberia. And he paid his dues at the Gulf Oil Refinery in Lake Charles until 1954, when a record promo man told him this: "You play too much accordion to be in these woods." And a king, the Swamp Boss, the man who would write the music's Magna Carta, was born. Clifton essentially invented modern zydeco, and after he was "discovered" in Houston in the 1960s, he earned the right to go through life as he did—with a blinding rack of gold incisors and gem-studded crowns and massive Hohner accordions. Clifton passed on to his bayou reward in 1987, but not before leaving the world that mad, dizzy, throbbing mix of blues, jazz, Creole, Cajun, and country stomp that was known as zydeco, zordico, and a million other names. It was a sound that came out of the Sweet Jesus Neverland somewhere on either side of the Sabine River . . . the swamp, the woods, the moist gumbo-earth place where it felt as if you and everyone else were walking on water . . . or quicksand . . . with the humidity so high it was like rain coming up from the ground . . . with the rubbery, endless, hypnotic backbeat that pressed down on you, held you, really held you, like some sort of sonic snake.

Tonight, Crown Prince Buckwheat is cradling his squeezebox, tilting his head back, and steering his band, Ils Sont Partis (French for "they're off," as it is shouted at the Acadiana Downs in Lafayette, Louisiana), through a slow, sweet, sexual musical confection. With the pace kicked down, it is easier to taste the individual zydeco ingredients, the things that make the *chank-a-chank-a-chank* beat, that skip across all boundaries from Houston R&B to East Texas country to Memphis soul. The saxophones. Gurgling guitars with that lulling, sweet-tempered, African melodic impulse. Gutbucket bass. And most of all, the corrugated steel rubboard and the thick, unyielding accordion mantra . . . as insistent, as repetitively rock steady as a 200-person gospel choir, the aural equivalent of trance dancing . . . the downbeat dervish, spinning and spinning and spinning around you, the same beat over and over again, until you are ready to handle snakes, the sonic snakes, until you are a southeast Texas Shaker, rocking with some primitive possession and speaking, muttering in some communal gumbo glossolalia.

Depending on who is telling the story and how late it is, you will learn the "snap bean" theory: the name "zydeco" traces back to *haricots*, the French word for snap beans, and an old tune about them. The extended theory is that people all dance, snap, and cook any way they like to that zydeco beat. This Saturday night, the dance floor is packed rump to rump, and a dizzying, un-church-like smell is in the air: cigarette smoke, stale perfume, sweat, liquor, gumbo, and sizzling pieces of pork cracklings. I can't help but stare at the crucifix planted on the wall behind Buckwheat's head. It has a No Smoking sign just below Jesus' feet.

As Big Man continues to make speeches, a hand plunks down two wet cans of cold beer in front of us. An elegant-looking guy in a natty suit smiles. "My treat," he says and disappears into the crowd of dancers.

"Who is he?" I ask Big Man.

"I don't know, but you were just dancing with his ugly wife," says Big Man.

In light of everything else this evening, I take the news in stride. All night at St. Peter's, I have been reacquainting myself with the peculiar kind of cultural bends a failed altar boy goes through when he plunges into Houston's—maybe Texas's—best-kept secret.

This Saturday night, turn the lights down low, bring your own cool beverages, eat home cookin' until you drop—it is the Catholic Church zydeco show.

"Every weekend you can hear a squeezebox at a church," offers Big Man.

He is sanctified and he is right.
Each weekend at one of a dozen different churches with mostly African American populations, the priests and nuns allow the parish gym halls to be possessed by a joyful noise unto the Lord. It is a hallowed custom imported straight to Texas from Louisiana's stomping grounds, and it seems to go back as long as anyone can remember. Ladies like Rose Thibodeaux, Edwina McGee, and Martha Boyance come in early Saturday afternoon and slap their supplies on the flat metal tables in the church cafeteria. In a few hours, they are engulfed in the swirling mists rising from simmering cauldrons of gumbo. "Chicken, sausage, shrimp, green onions, bell peppers, parsley, file, garlic salt," chants the round-faced Rose. The women debate the fine points of pinches, dollops, and handfuls of spices. Secret ingredients. Secret knowledge. Secret ways. Rose prefers to add two pieces

of fresh chicken to every bowl she serves, so the poultry situation needs to be addressed right away.

Other church ladies arrive with mounds of boudin, the translucent casings bulging to the size of a fat baby's arm. Somebody has the ancient recipe for frying the pork cracklings to just the right crunchiness. Big garbage cans are filled with ice and beer. And if you are truly blessed, as I was one night at St. Philip Neri Catholic Church, jolly nuns will be busy baking big platters of homemade sweet-potato pies (hopefully, made with the best yams in Texas, from Freestone County) that they will send down, still warm, from the convent next door.

Meanwhile, the churchmen do the manly things. They hang up neon beer signs underneath the basketball hoops. Set up folding chairs and drape the long card tables in plastic. Test the microphones and speakers more than they really need to be tested. Get more ice and more beer. Mill around a lot, drink the now cold beer, watch the women do the real work, and argue about why the smoothly talented but hardheaded Rockin' Sidney, born in tiny Lebeau in St. Landry Parish, dropped off the Texas Catholic Church circuit for so long . . . and whether Houston's earnest Wilbert Thibodeaux and his Zydeco Rascals are really worth listening to. (They are.)

"We're in charge of making sure the music gets here," the leather-jacketed and also physically huge Freddie Sam tells me as he stands in the back of the St. Peter the Apostle hall. Freddie has been helping out on the Catholic zydeco scene for years. Like dozens of people I meet, he still has family ringing either side of Bayou Teche, a musical breeding ground that runs from Opelousas south to Morgan City and that so many southeast Texans trace their roots, their blood, to. Freddie says he is somewhat related to the very cool Sam Brothers Five and their immortal father, a former fixture on the Houston scene, accordionist Herbert "Good Rocking" Sam. Freddie is also a member of one of the zydeco committees that the Catholics rely on to coordinate the different shows. Over the years, scheduling conflicts among the dozen churches that regularly sponsor dances caused the crowds—and the profits—to be split up. One church would inadvertently schedule John Delafose and his Eunice Playboys the same weekend that traditionalists Boozoo Chavis (whose gift to the universe is the classic "Paper in My Shoe") would be at a church on the other side of town. *And what was a good zydeco Catholic to do?*

The zydeco bigwigs at each church finally called a truce. Meetings were held and a nonconflicting schedule was set up. Now the way things have been working, only one of the churches in the zydeco network will have a dance each weekend. The churches have to worry about competing with one another only during baseball season. "We didn't want no fuss," says deep-voiced Nolan Thibodeaux (attend any of the dances and you will run into plenty of people named Thibodeaux), who is a leader of the zydeco panel at St. Philip Neri.

No fuss.

I listen to Edwina McGee, who came to Houston from south Louisiana in the early 1950s, and hear an extension of that theme. The Catholic Church zydeco show revolves around minimizing hassles. People of all ages come to the church zydeco show because they can do everything they can at a night-club—smoke, drink, and tell lies in the name of love—and they can do it under the relative safety of the Big Church Umbrella. "People who come here aren't looking for trouble. If they are, they go someplace else," the angel-faced Edwina tells me late one evening. "And when they dance, everyone just does their own thing. Don't matter what anyone else is doing, you do your own thing."

In mid-inspection of the gumbo pot, Edwina suddenly wants to know whether there are any zydeco churches in Dallas. I tell her the city is full of Baptists who don't dance. (For an unholy second, I thought about telling her the joke I heard from a Baptist missionary. "Why don't Baptists make love standing up?" Answer: "Because they are afraid someone will think they are dancing.") All of which leads the conversation to the salient point of the Catholic zydeco experience. From the glowing Lowenbrau sign to the little swizzle sticks, it really is no different from being in Club LaVeek on Blodgett, in Houston, or The Web Lounge in San Antonio. So is this any way for a church in Texas to behave?

"Of course it is," says Rose Thibodeaux. "You can go hide in the closet and have a nip if you want. But we're a little more honest about it. Every-thing in the world is there for a purpose, and there's nothing wrong with having a little fun."

Listening to her friend, Martha Boyance nods her head and watches me break another package of saltines into my gumbo bowl. ("Crackers is a Texas thing. Texas people like those crackers," insists Edwina.)

"People will do anything in the world to get these dances," claims Martha, who introduces herself to strangers by saying, "I'm French." A slender, small sixty-eight-year-old woman with an angular face, her family's roots are in Decalmbre, Louisiana, close to New Iberia. Her family saga resembles doz-ens you can hear described at any of the church functions. Her father was an "attendant" to a doctor, and he was also a man who "was very, very mixy with the white people." The family, like many of the other African American families in south Louisiana, was chronically short of money and clothing, but never short of food. There were sweet potatoes, peanuts, corn, butter, milk, couscous, sugar cane syrup, smothered turtle, and garfish. "We'd walk four or five miles on a Sunday afternoon into the woods. We carried the lemonade and the food, and we'd have a country dance or a church dance," remembers Martha. "Everybody was related back then. Know what I mean? Everybody was your cousin. We just called each other cousin."

Over the decades, families like Martha's migrated to the big city of Houston, chasing down the same universal goals: better jobs, better schools, better futures. When they left for Houston, the church dances came along with them. People at St. Peter's remember them being held in Houston back in the 1930s, and several of them say they surely go back much further. "They've been doing it forever," insists Martha.

B y ten, the good cooks are braced for business.
The lights are being turned down low. Rose and Edwina slide dishes of food out of the little cafeteria window. Buckwheat is patrolling the stage, the American flag to one side, the Lone Star to the other. The little metal ashtrays are already overflowing with stubs. Ubiquitous bottles of Crown Royal, Tanqueray, and the other superlatively cool staples of the down-home circuit are being uncorked.

"I feel like a lemon waiting for a squeeze," screams one of Freddie Sam's friends. "I want to la-la tonight!"

He puts his head close to Freddie's, and the men ramble on in French, giggle, and shout some more about how they are both from "Bigfoot country." And without missing a beat, they begin praising the names of the parish priests at St. Peter's. "They will walk off to one side with you," whispers Freddie. "They give you courage, strength, and faith to go on. Sometimes they come to my house and give my wife her last rites."

Freddie's wife has been at death's door. She can't make it to the dances anymore. He comes out by himself, sees friends, collects the admission money, and occasionally gets up to squeeze his way onto the dance floor. Like a lot of big men, he has a surprising John Belushi–John Candy nimbleness about him, to go with this Sylvester the Cat grin. All evening he slips in and out of the shadows, a slightly sad smile on his face and his fingers waving a little kid's goodbye. "I feel my hips. They're talking to me," says Freddie.

Onstage, Buckwheat is flipping his patented south Louisiana, refried James Brown Dippity-Do hairdo back and forth. He has downshifted into a slippery and moist version of Bobby Charles's "Walking to New Orleans." Buckwheat is zooted out in white boots, purple suit, and ruffled shirt. His squeezebox is the largest one in the world, a cream-colored thing with a dark center that slowly yawns open when he spreads his arms apart. Every time he fans the accordion out, his face twists up with a mad kind of joy. Through the cigarette haze, it all looks vaguely obscene and totally, irresistibly impossible to ignore—like strolling in front of the sex-on-display windows in Amsterdam, Berlin, or, for that matter, New Orleans. The crowd has a chanting response to every move that Buckwheat makes: "Yeahum-uh-hah, yeahum-uh-hah, yeahum-uh-hah."

From each corner of the high-ceilinged church hall, there is a call and response. The church ladies were right: people are doing their own thing. Modified, rock-me-like-my-back-has-no-bone versions of the Watusi. A couple of two-steppers. A birthday-party conga line.

A backstage door suddenly opens, and a thin ray of light spills across the church stage. It is a sacred moment. Buckwheat, the Neal Cassady of the accordion, beams out at the Merry Pranksters who have clambered aboard his zydeco express. "This is a trip," he proudly announces to the throbbing audience.

The exalted grand knight of the Knights of Peter Claver is pressed against a far back wall of a rival church, St. Peter the Apostle. Calvin A. Donatto is in a suit, dressed like a diplomat, like a respected emissary, which he is. And he is explaining how the Houston Zydeco Board has saved the churches from each other, and how the French-speaking African Americans in this part of Texas have tried to save their roots.

"Most of the people who come to these things still speak a bit of French," Donatto tells me. As he waves his hands, the trusty churchmen are rolling in new garbage cans crammed with melting ice and cans of Miller. "My grandfather spoke French all the time, just like the people from Frenchtown." Frenchtown for many folks remains the area around the venerable and arguably best barbecue palace in the history of Houston, the smoke-scarred Lockwood Inn at Lockwood and Interstate 10. For decades, the Semien family's gorgeous caramel-colored daughters served up sausage created according to heaven's own recipe; Howard Hughes was a regular, and so were the ship-channel hipsters, grifters, and sailors.

The continuing connection, the blurring of lines, between Houston and south Louisiana was once easy to find all over the city. Before Hurricane Katrina forced thousands of refugees into Houston, there was a long, long musical-religious-culinary connection. The Continental Lounge was a major zydeco institution for years, and the only place, other than Katmandu, Nepal, where someone approached me and asked for money "to watch" my means of transportation after I had parked it (in Nepal, they asked me for money to watch my parked bicycle—"bicycle looking," it was called). I gladly paid the five dollars the guy was asking outside the Continental. And why not? My car was always there when I left the club.

One of America's premier musicologists, Houston's Mack McCormick, is generally credited with giving the world the accepted spelling of "zydeco." And people still talk about the historical string of restaurants, clubs, and icehouses that catered to that African American–Creole community: The Satellite, Cepanso, Monroe's, Mr. V's, Club Razzmatazz. But in the end, people credit the Catholic Church with being the real glue that allowed the French zydeco community in Texas to bend and not break. "With integration, the French society began to break up," explains Donatto. "Old restaurants went away. Clubs closed down. But these church dances give everyone an opportunity to get back together. It's like being a member of a club. You speak French, and everyone knows each other. We go from church to church every weekend."

And they do.

Yet one more very large man, this one in snakeskin boots, is ushering me into what looks like a pitch-black confessional.

It is one in the morning, and I am hoping Buckwheat is somewhere in this dark quiet place somewhere in the rear of the St. Peter the Apostle church hall.

All evening and into the early morning, Stanley Durel, Jr., who changed his name to Buckwheat Zydeco after blending his love for the Little Rascals with his respect for Clifton Chenier, has been alternatively exorcising demons and raising hell. He has worked the crowd like Jerry Lee Lewis filtered through Jimmy Swaggart. Crying, pleading, wailing on bended knee. The screaming imam of zydeco, he has called the faithful home in any number of ways. Like James Brown used to do, Buckwheat has shown that he can play the organ. He has gone to the floor and led the crowd in another "Zydeco-go-here, go-here, go-here." He has hooked up some sort of portable synthesizer to a wiggling surgical tube and forced hard-core Memphis-Stax-soul music out of it. And now, he has given his band of disciples, dripping in sweat, a break.

From the right-hand corner of the closet I am in, there comes a scratchy, almost weary voice: "I tell you, a good washboard player is so very hard to find."

Buckwheat comes into focus. He is sitting on a folding chair, a beer in one hand and a plastic cup with something else in it resting at his feet. His down mood lasts for just a second. He is suddenly filled with the same energy he had on stage, with words and thoughts tumbling out the same way people rush to the dance floor when he plays the opening strains of "I Bought a Raccoon."

He is, in the end, the imam-priest-rabbi who had to carry the accordion torch now that Clifton Chenier has sailed to zydeco heaven. As he talks, it becomes clear that his mentor gave more than just his holy robes to his protégé. Buckwheat Zydeco has a zealot's grasp of the clear truths in the music, and why the Catholic Church zydeco celebrations are so important. "I stayed away from that accordion for years. It was old. I didn't want anything to do with it," he admits to me. "Then Clifton called me one day. He said, 'Buckwheat, that accordion has been there waiting for you, it is your roots, it has power and energy.'"

He still defers to Clifton as the king—"then, now, and tomorrow." But zydeco has been good to Buckwheat. It has taken him around the world, and he has never looked back, except to worship at the altar of his roots. Stevie Ray Vaughan, the great white blues guitarist from Oak Cliff, Texas, once told someone that he was learning "to pray" through his guitar. Buckwheat was praying and preaching.

"Playing the church halls is like playing home," he tells me as we sit in the dark. It is, really, like being in a confessional, all shadows, mysteries, and blind faith. Purity really is hard to find.

"It's pure. There aren't too many things you can call pure anymore."

Yeahum-uh-hah, yeahum-uh-hah, yeahum-uh-hah.

Buckwheat Zydeco travels the world with his accordion. A few clubs have come and gone, or changed names, but the church zydeco scene remains the rock in Texas.

CREDITS

Thank you to the publishers and editors who graciously granted permission to reprint the stories in this collection.

"Texas Harlem Blues" originally appeared as "Percy Sutton—The Texas-bred Politico Is Still the Toast of Harlem," *Dallas Morning News*, August 13, 1995.

"Black Panther Blues" originally appeared as "Fahim Minkah's Uneasy Mission—Crack Cocaine Is the Enemy," *Dallas Morning News*, September 3, 1989, and "The Fire Man," *Dallas Morning News*, July 21, 1991.

"Hanging Tree Blues" originally appeared as "Remembering Where He Has Been . . . Enables Ray Rhodes to Get Where He Is Going," *Sporting News*, September 30, 1996.

"Congo Street Blues" originally appeared as "Congo Street—In the Shadow of Fair Park, a Neighborhood Lives with the Labels of the Past," *Dallas Morning News*, November 14, 1987.

"Free Man Blues" originally appeared as "The Town That Time Forgot—Tucked Away in the Woods, the Freedmen's Town of Joppa Is Modest and Used to Doing Things for Itself," *Dallas Morning News*, October 10, 1993.

"Sand Branch Blues" originally appeared as "The Bottom—For Decades, Dallas Development Has Claimed the Good Earth of Sandbranch," *Dallas Morning News*, September 15, 1991.

"Fire in the Hole Blues" originally appeared as "The Hole—Whether They

Come for 'Catch Out' Work or Warm Words, They Find a Sense of Family around the Fire Barrel," *Dallas Morning News*, April 18, 1993.

"South Dallas Blues" originally appeared as "In Search of Common Ground—Fear and Frustration: The Residents' Perspective," *Dallas Morning News*, March 29, 1987.

"Photochemical Blues" originally appeared as "Blues Elegy," *Dallas Morning News*, February 26, 1989.

"Searchin' Blues" originally appeared as "In Search of the Blues—With Roots Firmly Planted in the Trinity River Bottoms, the Music Thrives in Nightspots from Booker's Arandas on Oakland Avenue to Fort Worth's Bluebird," *Dallas Morning News*, February 7, 1988.

"Last Man Blues" originally appeared as "The Last True Texas Bluesman—How a Farmer and Mechanic from Tiny Elmo, Texas, Wound Up on a Road to the Recording Studio, Nightclubs and European Music Festivals," *Dallas Morning News*, April 17, 1994.

"Lightnin' Blues" originally appeared as "Saying Goodbye," *Houston Chronicle*, February 7, 1982.

"Chicken Shack Blues" originally appeared as "Singin' the Blues: Amos Milburn Was a Black Bluesman Who Walked Tall and Lived Good but Died Quiet," *Houston Chronicle*, February 12, 1982.

"Fourth Ward Blues" originally appeared as "King of Fourth Ward's Influential Roadside Music Comes On Home," *Houston Chronicle*, June 20, 1982.

"Zydeco Blues" originally appeared as "La-La Tonight! Squeezin' and Pleasin' on the Zydeco Church Circuit," *Houston Press*, January 11, 1990.